the Tasty Greek Recipes *of* Cyprus

THE TASTY GREEK SONG - My Story

CHORUS
HE IS THE TASTY GREEK
HE IS THE TASTY GREEK
HE WANTS TO TELL YOU SOMETHING ABOUT THE FOOD HE LIKES TO EAT

VERSE 1
MY STORY IS NOT TOO LONG
IT'S RATHER SHORT AND SWEET
IT'S ALL ABOUT MY GREEK FOOD
CAUSE IT GOES DOWN QUITE A TREAT
MY MAMA SAID, A NICO
COME AND HELP ME COOK
I WRITE DOWN ALL THE RECIPES
AND MAKE A GREEK COOKBOOK

**Listen to the song
log onto
www.thetastygreek.com**

VERSE 2
YOUR FIND THIS FOOD IS DIFFERENT
FROM THE FOOD YOU'VE HAD BEFORE
BUT ONCE YOU'VE COOKED AND ATE IT
YOUR BE COMING BACK FOR MORE
THE METHODS ARE LAID OUT EASY
EVEN A NOVICE CAN LEARN TO COOK
SO WHY NOT TRY THE REAL MOUSSAKA
WHEN YOU BUY THIS BOOK

VERSE 3
MY FAVOURITE IS SOUVLAKI
I RECOMMEND TO YOU
IT SMELLS AND TASTES SO LOVELY
COOKED ON THE BBQ
I EAT IT WITH A SALAD
AND SOME TOASTED PITAS TOO
ADD A RICE PILAVI
IT'S VERY GOOD FOR YOU

VERSE 4
PLEASE DON'T YOU DISAPPOINT ME
TRY THIS GASTRONOMIC TREAT
I'VE CATERED FOR VEGETARIANS
AND THOSE WHO LIKE TO EAT MEAT
SO ENJOY IT WITH SOME OUZO
AND YOUR BE DANCING ON YOUR FEET
I BET YOU'RE WANDERING WHO I AM
I'M NICO, THE TASTY GREEK

Nicholas
Adam

Nicolaou

This is a (The Tasty Greek Publications Book)
First Published in 2004

Copyright © Nicholas Adam Nicolaou 2000

Designed and Produced by
Nick Nicolaou

Photographs by
Nick Nicolaou
Nicola Nicolaou
Michael Nicolaou
Emma Wee
Eagle Studio

Illustrated - Poetry by
Nick Nicolaou

Song by
Nick Nicolaou
Adam Nicolaou

Logo Design by
Nick Nicolaou
Michael Nicolaou
Adam Nicolaou

ISBN 0-9544346-0-9

British Library Cataloguing in Publication Data.
A catalogue record for this book is available from the British Library.

The Tasty Greek Publications
P.O.BOX 38474
LONDON
SE16 6YZ

www.thetastygreek.com

Printed by Colchester Print Group

Printed and bound in the United Kingdom.

I dedicate this book to my mum, Despina for sharing her time, knowledge and the delicious recipes that make up this book.

ACKNOWLEDGEMENTS

I like to thank the following people: -

Nicola - Adam - Michael Nicolaou
Natasa (Soula) Zafiriou, Chris Theodorou,
John Hennessy, Joseph Maw, Simba, Ian Cole,
Gary Wells, Will Paterson,
Patrick & Catherine McLoughlin

Karen Mandeville, Stefan Berber, Hena Patel at
Southwark College

John Riches, Tom Deveson, Emma Wee, at
English National Opera

Renie Coffey, of
CanView

not forgetting my dog: Basil

The Tasty Greek

Contents

Introduction

to the Tasty Greek

I come from a Greek Cypriot background and at a young age I was left to provide and become the father figure to the family. I left school with very few qualifications and went on to have a varied working career. I started in a wholesale tailoring manufacturer and later went on to work as a plastering sub-contractor, a manager for a nation-wide electrical store, a warehouse supervisor for a marine company, a vault supervisor for a security storage company - successfully passed all necessary exams along the way.

There is no limit to my versatility and thirst for turning my hands to new projects and ventures. Having an interest for theatre - in 2001, I performed with my son Michael in a community project "South of the River" a non-opera production with the English National Opera. In 2003 I played a supporting role to the actors and actresses in Southwark: _the Movie_ in aid of raising money for a charitable Trust. Furthermore, I've attended Southwark College for computer graphics and desktop publishing. Food preparation catering classes to qualify as a chef; I feel it is an important part to this work – since I am writing a cookbook. I have also written a number of poems to accompany this book and a song (My Story) that can be listened to by logging onto _the Tasty Greek_ website.

Finally, I dedicate this book to my mother for sharing her delicious recipes which enabled me to write this Greek Cypriot cookbook of home-made, easy to cook, no nonsense tried and tested recipes using very nutritious and healthy ingredients for a gastronomic treat catering for meat eaters and vegetarians. The recipes I have covered in my book are the most frequently used in Greek Cypriot Cuisine and I know you will enjoy them as much as I do.

Cheers! - stin iya sas, is iyian!

"I have known Nicholas and his mother Despina for many years. I have admired her delicious cooking as it reminds me so much of home and the wonderful food from Cyprus. I was very excited to hear that Nicholas was putting all these lovely recipes down in a book for us all to share."
Natasa (Soula) Zafiriou.
Actress - Singer.

"If Nick brings as much commitment, skill and thoughtfulness to his cooking as he did to acting, singing, and dancing in *South of the River*, we're in for a gastronomic treat!"
John Riches
Co-ordinator, English National Opera's North Southwark Programme.

Nick Nicolaou is a great enthusiast. In the Southwark community opera, South of the River, he threw himself into acting and singing and made every kind of commitment to ensure that the opera would be a success. He communicated his enthusiasm to colleagues, friends and neighbours, helping to create an audience as well as a show for them to come and see.

He is also an enthusiast for Greek cuisine. He knows how it's developed and he knows how it should be done. He likes making, eating and serving the food and he wants others to share in his enjoyment. The opera was a feast for the eyes and ears and Nick's book should create a feast for the taste buds.
Tom Deveson
Advisory teacher for Music, Southwark LEA (1999).

Information for the Reader

Wash hands and all produce before preparation.

Spoon measures are level, unless otherwise specified.

Measures in the recipes are given in metric, for the best results follow the recipes.

Conversion tables are approximate only and have been rounded up or down.

Oven temperatures and cooking times will vary according to the equipment and the size, quality and type of ingredients / food used. Always refer to your cooking instruction book.

Eggs are a medium size and of an average weight of about 60g.

Lemons are of medium size having an average weight of about 100g. Use fresh lemon juice.

Colocassi (large) are of an average weight of about 750g.

Aubergines are of an average weight of about 350g.

Courgettes are of an average weight of about 250g.

Bell peppers are of an average weight of about 175g.

Bread yeast is dried fast action from a sachet (7g per sachet).

Bread dough should be made slightly wet but not sticky, this gives the bread a softer loaf.

To peel fresh tomatoes use a sharp knife to cut out the core from the top and then slice a shallow cross at the bottom. Immerse the tomatoes in boiling water for 20 seconds then transfer to a bowl of cold water using a slotted spoon. As soon as the tomatoes are cool enough to handle, use the side of the knife blade or your fingers to peel off the skin.

Jars must be of good condition with an affective seal. Sterilise jars using recommended tablets from (pharmacist) or carefully place in boiling water for 5 minutes and then thoroughly dry.

Dips, I recommend you make the dips at least two to three hours before serving to allow the flavours to develop.

Conversion Tables

DRY WEIGHT CONVERSIONS

IMPERIAL	METRIC
1/4 oz	7 g
1/2 oz	15 g
1 oz	25 g
2 oz	50 g
3 oz	75 g
4 oz (1/4 lb)	110 g
5 oz	150 g
6 oz	175 g
7 oz	200 g
8 oz (1/2 lb)	225 g
9 oz	250 g
10 oz	275 g
11 oz	300 g
12 oz (3/4 lb)	340 g
13 oz	375 g
14 oz	400 g
15 oz	425 g
16 oz (1 lb)	450 g
1 1/4 lb	560 g
1 1/2 lb	680 g
1 3/4 lb	800 g
2 lb	900 g
2 1/2 lb	1125 g
3 lb	1360 g
3 1/2 lb	1600 g
4 lb	1800 g
4 1/2 lb	2000 g (2 kg)
5 lb	2265 g

MEASUREMENTS ARE APPROXIMATE EQUIVALENT ONLY

568 ml = 1 UK pint

16 fl oz = 1 US pint

Helpful Measurements

Metric	Imperial
6 mm	1/4 in
1 cm	1/2 in
2 cm	1 in
4 cm	1 1/2 in
5 cm	2 in
6 cm	2 1/2 in
8 cm	3 in
10 cm	4 in
13 cm	5 in
15 cm	6 in
16 cm	6 1/2 in
18 cm	7 in
20 cm	8 in
23 cm	9 in
25 cm	10 in
30 cm	12 in (1 ft)

LIQUID CONVERSIONS

IMPERIAL	METRIC
1/2 fl oz	15 ml
1 fl oz	30 ml
2 fl oz	60 ml (1/4 cup)
3 fl oz	90 ml
4 fl oz	125 ml (1/2 cup)
5 fl oz (1/4 pt)	150 ml
6 fl oz	175 ml
7 fl oz	210 ml
8 fl oz	250 ml (1 cup)
9 fl oz	275 ml
10 fl oz (1/2 pt)	300 ml
11 fl oz	340 ml
12 fl oz	375 ml (1 1/2 cups)
16 fl oz	500 ml (2 cups)
20 fl oz (1 pt)	600 ml
1 1/2 pints	900 ml
1 3/4 pints	1 litre (4 cups)
2 pints	1 1/4 litres
2 1/3 pints	1 1/2 litres
3 1/4 pints	2 litres
4 1/4 pints	2 1/2 litres
5 pints	3 litres

Conventional Electric °F	°C	Fan Oven °C	Gas Mark	cool | Very Hot
200	100	80	1/4	very low / slow / cool
225	110	90	1/4	very low / slow / cool
250	130	110	1/2	low / slow
275	140	120	1	low / slow
300	150	130	2	low / slow
325	160	140	3	moderate low
350	180	160	4	moderate / medium
375	190	180	5	moderate hot
400	200	190	6	hot
425	220	200	7	hot / high
450	230	210	8	very hot
500	250	220	9	very hot

Abbreviations and Symbols

oz = ounces, lb = pounds, g = grammes, kg = kilogrammes
fl oz = fluid ounces, pt = pints, ml = millilitres, lt = litres
mm = millimetres, cm = centimetres, in = inches, ft = feet

tsp = teaspoons, tbsp = tablespoons
1 level teaspoon = 5 ml
1 level tablespoon = 15 ml
1 tablespoon = 3 teaspoons

°F = Fahrenheit, °C = Celsius

dips

Simply add the ingredients to a mixing bowl,
Blend it, mix it, work it - but not too much or it ends up
looking like smooth bread dough,
Make no excuses and invite round some friends,
Let them dip in to the very end.

soups

Cold days are a recipe for hot soups,
Warming and circulating right down to your boots,
Eat them slow and feel your body glow - but don't you
dare slurp,
Cause your follow it with an almighty burp.

salads

Tease your taste buds with a crunch and a chew,
That's what a Greek salad is supposed to do,
Ideal to eat on a hot summers night,
Accompanied with anything it makes a refreshing bite.

FETA TYRI SALATA

(Feta Cheese Dip)

This dip is less well known than the other popular varieties. I use a fork to mix the ingredients together so as not to over work the dip, it should not be smooth and can be made a day ahead, cover with cling film and refrigerate.

Serves 4 to 6.

200g of plain Greek yogurt
100g of feta cheese, crumbled
3 tablespoons of double cream
1 fat clove of garlic, crushed
1 tablespoon of fresh lemon thyme, finely chopped
2 tablespoons of lemon juice
salt to taste

Combine the yogurt, cheese, cream, garlic, lemon thyme and lemon juice into a bowl. Mix well. Add salt to taste and serve.

TARAMASALATA

(Fish Egg Dip)

Salted mullet roe was traditionally the true tarama, and which it derives its name. Smoked cod roe is my favoured choice for this recipe, I find it produces a lovely creamy texture. If you prefer this dip pink in colour, a teaspoon of beetroot juice can be added. If the dip is too thick a small amount of water can be added. I use Greek bread that's been left out 2 to 3 days but any stale bread can be used. The dip can be made a day ahead, cover with cling film and refrigerate.

Serves 4 to 6.

200g of smoked cod roe
3 slices of stale bread (crust removed and soaked in a small bowl of water for
1 minute then squeezed)
1 tablespoon of fresh curly parsley, finely chopped
1 clove of garlic, crushed
juice of half a lemon
125 ml of extra virgin olive oil
salt to taste

Remove roe from its membrane and place into a food processor. Add the bread, parsley, garlic and lemon juice. Blitz until thick and creamy. While the processor is operating, add the olive oil in a thin stream until it is combined together. Taste and add salt if required.

Tips
If smoked cod roe is unavailable, ask your fishmonger for a suitable alternative.

TAHINI

(Sesame Seed Dip)

Tahini paste is roasted and pulped sesame seed. It is readily available and can be bought in jars at most food stores. This might seem the easiest dip to make but can be the trickiest, because it's all down to the amount of water used. Experiment and have fun, it should turn out smooth and not too sticky when made. The dip can be made a day ahead, cover with cling film and refrigerate.

Serves 4 to 6.

175 ml of tahini paste
2 clove of garlic, crushed
juice of 1 lemon
2 tablespoons of extra virgin olive oil
120 ml of water
salt to taste

Combine the tahini paste, garlic, lemon juice and olive oil in a bowl. Mix well then add the water a little at a time to make a smooth texture. Add salt to taste and serve.

TZATZIKI

(Yogurt and Cucumber Dip)

Another well-known dip that tastes much better home made. Any cucumber variety of your choice can be used. The dip can be made a day ahead, cover with cling film and refrigerate. This dip is an ideal accompaniment to the kreas souvlakia.

<u>Serves 4 to 6.</u>

500g of plain Greek yogurt
1 cucumber of about 30 cm long (12 inch)
seeds removed and chopped into small cubes **or** grated
4 tablespoons of fresh mint, finely chopped
1 fat clove of garlic, crushed
2 tablespoons of lemon juice
3 tablespoons of extra virgin olive oil
salt to taste

Combine the yogurt, cucumber, mint, garlic, lemon juice and olive oil in a bowl. Mix well. Add salt to taste and serve.

HOUMOUS

(Chick Pea Dip)

Tinned chick peas are used in this recipe for simplicity and quickness. Dried chick peas can be used but must be soaked overnight in cold water and can take up to two hours of cooking. The dip can be made a day ahead, cover with cling film and refrigerate.

Serves 4 to 6.

410g tin of chick peas, drained
100g of tahini paste
3 cloves of garlic
juice of half a lemon
100 ml of extra virgin olive oil (plus 1 tablespoon to garnish)
enough water to bring to a paste
salt to taste
1 tablespoon of fresh flat leaf parsley, finely chopped (to garnish)

Pour the chick peas into a food processor and process until pulped. Add the tahini paste, garlic, lemon juice and olive oil. Process for 30 seconds while adding the water to make a slightly smooth texture. Add salt to taste. Drizzle over the tablespoon of olive oil and sprinkle with the flat leaf parsley to serve.

ELIES MEH SKORTHO

(Marinated Olives)

The best time to buy fresh olives is in the autumn when they are at their best. I have used green olives for this recipe, which are in fact unripe ones. Make sure you buy them from a good Mediterranean food shop where you are allowed to choose the olives for yourself.

Makes 1 jar.

1 kg of fresh green olives, cracked
enough water for soaking
preserving marinade
100g of salt
$1\frac{1}{4}$ litres of water
2 cloves of garlic, chopped
1 teaspoon of coriander seeds, lightly crushed
1 lemon, sliced
sealing the olives
enough olive oil to cover the olives (about 2 cm deep)

Discard any blemished olives. Place olives into a plastic bag in batches. Using a rolling pin carefully crack the olives. Add all the cracked olives to a sterilised jar (2-litre capacity). Cover with water to about 5 cm from the top. Scum will appear on the surface of the water. Change the water in the jar every day for 7 days. Combine the salt and the $1\frac{1}{4}$ litres of water, stir until the salt dissolves. Drain the water from the jar and then pour in enough salted water to completely cover the olives. Add the garlic, coriander seeds and lemon slices. Pour the olive oil into the jar and seal completely. Label and date the jar. Store in a cool, dry, dark place for 4 weeks before use.

Tips
These olives make a very nice paste, when stoned and blitzed in a food processor.

SALATA MEH PATATES

(Greek Salad with Potatoes)

The cucumbers used in the recipe are of the slender young green variety about 15 to 20 cm long (6-8 inches) and have a slight sweet taste and a crisp sound when snapped in half. Usually found in fruit and vegetable markets and in most Mediterranean shops.

Serves 4 to 6.

500g of new potatoes
half a cos lettuce, shredded
quarter of white cabbage, core removed and shredded
3 medium tomatoes, cut into eighths (small wedges)
2 slender green cucumbers, quartered and thickly sliced
6 spring onions, cut into 1 cm pieces
2 tablespoons of fresh coriander, finely chopped
dressing
juice of half a lemon
4 tablespoons of extra virgin olive oil
salt to taste

Place the potatoes into a saucepan and cover with cold water. Bring to the boil then simmer until the potatoes are tender. Drain and set aside to go cold then peel and cut into quarters. In a large bowl combine the potatoes, lettuce, cabbage, tomatoes, cucumbers, onions and coriander. Drizzle the salad with lemon juice and olive oil and mix together to coat. Add salt to taste and serve.

SALATA MEH ELIES KEH FETA

(Greek Salad)

I have purposely left out the use of herbs as the feta cheese and olives are strong in taste. The cucumbers used in the recipe are of the slender young green variety about 15 to 20 cm long (6-8 inches) and have a slight sweet taste and a crisp sound when snapped in half. Usually found in fruit and vegetable markets and in most Mediterranean shops.

Serves 4 to 6.

1 cos lettuce, shredded
3 medium tomatoes, cut into eighths (small wedges)
2 slender green cucumbers, quartered and thickly sliced
6 spring onions, cut into 1 cm pieces
110g of pitted black olives
200g of feta cheese, crumbled or cubed
dressing
juice of half a lemon
4 tablespoons of extra virgin olive oil
salt to taste

In a large bowl combine the lettuce, tomatoes, cucumbers, onions, olives and cheese. Drizzle the salad with lemon juice and olive oil and mix together to coat. Add salt to taste and serve.

Tips
Alternatively, put the 200g of feta cheese in a baking dish, warm through in the oven and place on top of the salad. Leave the olives out, if they are not to your taste.

FASOULATHA SOOPA

(Vegetables and Butter Bean Soup)

This soup is very popular and butter beans give a lovely creamy texture. In this recipe I have used tinned butter beans for simplicity, as they are so readily available nowadays. Best served with a sprinkle of flat leaf parsley and a big chunk of crusty bread.

<u>Serves 4 to 6.</u>

8 new potatoes, peeled and cut in half
3 carrots, sliced
3 sticks of celery, sliced
1 medium onion, sliced
1 1/2 litres of water
500g of fresh tomatoes, peeled and chopped <u>or</u> 400g tin of tomatoes, chopped
1 teaspoon of tomato purée
1 chicken or vegetable stock cube
2 tablespoons of extra virgin olive oil
1 teaspoon of salt
2 x 400g tins of butter beans (drained and washed)

Put the potatoes, carrots, celery and onion into a large saucepan and cover with the cold water. Bring to the boil, and then simmer until all the vegetables are just tender. Add the tomatoes, tomato purée, stock cube, olive oil and salt. Stir and continue to cook for a further 15 minutes. Add the butter beans and simmer for 5 minutes then serve.

<u>Tips</u>
Alternatively, any medium size bean can be used. If using dried beans always cook as directed on the packet.

TRAHANA SOOPA

(Yogurt Soaked Cracked Wheat Soup)

Trahana is cracked wheat soaked in plain Greek yogurt and dried into small uneven shaped pieces. This soup is an acquired taste as it is slightly sour, but the halloumi cheese helps to take away some of the sourness. The cracked wheat expands when soaked in water.

Serves 4 to 6.

250g of trahana
2$1/2$ litres of water
1 medium tomato, roughly chopped
2 tablespoons of sunflower oil
125g of halloumi cheese, roughly chopped

Place the cracked wheat and water into a large saucepan. Cover and leave to soak for 2 hours. Bring to the boil, then simmer gently for 30 minutes. In another saucepan, fry the tomato in the sunflower oil until soft then add to the soup. Add the halloumi cheese and stir well. Continue to cook on a low heat for a further 20 minutes. Remove from the heat and let it rest for 10 minutes to allow the soup to thicken before serving.

Tips
The cracked wheat (Trahana) can be purchased from most Mediterranean green grocers.

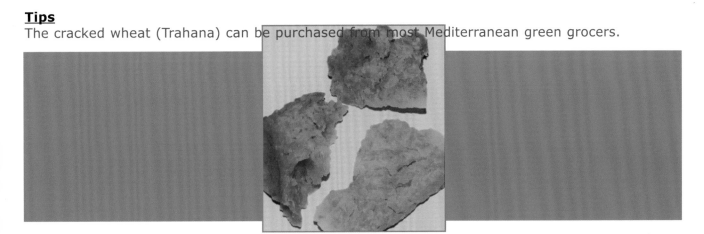

ROOVITI SOOPA

(Chick Pea Soup)

If you like chick peas this soup is a must, because as you bite into the peas you get a lovely crunchy texture to a buttery flavour. Along with the juice it's just so delicious and very simple to make.

Serves 4 to 6.

500g of dried chick peas
1 1/2 litres of water
1 vegetable or chicken stock cube
1 teaspoon of salt
2 medium onions, sliced
4 tablespoons of extra virgin olive oil
500g of fresh tomatoes, peeled and chopped **or** 400g tin of tomatoes, chopped

Cook the chick peas as directed on the packet. Drain then add the water, stock cube and salt, bring back to the boil then simmer. In another saucepan fry the onions in the olive oil until soft, add the tomatoes and cook for 3 minutes then pour the sauce into the chick peas and stir. Simmer for a further 15 minutes then serve.

PSARI SOOPA

(Fish Soup)

I like to use sea bass for this recipe as I like the creamy white rich texture of the flesh but any fish of your choice can be used. This fish soup is an alternative to the meat soup for those who do not eat meat or just fancy a change.

Serves 4 to 6.

1 sea bass, cleaned and about 700g in weight
$2_{1/2}$ litres of water
150g of long grain rice
4 medium potatoes, peeled and quartered
1 medium onion, sliced
3 carrots, sliced
2 leeks, sliced
3 sticks of celery, sliced
3 tablespoons of fresh flat leaf parsley, chopped
1 clove of garlic, crushed (optional)
half a tablespoon of salt
1 large pinch of ground black pepper

In a large saucepan simmer the fish in the water until cooked through, skimming off any froth that appears then remove the fish and set aside. Strain the stock to remove any bones. Bring the stock back to the boil then add the rice, potatoes, onion, carrots, leeks, celery, parsley, garlic, (if using) salt and pepper. Simmer and cook until the rice and potatoes are tender. Remove the fish from the bone and return to the soup. Continue to simmer for 5 minutes or until the fish is hot then serve.

Tips
To make a creamier soup, mix 2 eggs and the juice of 1 lemon in a bowl, add a little of the soup juice (if too hot, eggs will scramble) then pour into the soup and mix well.
Fishmongers will usually clean whole fish ready for cooking.

MAKARONIA KEH KOTOPOULO SOOPA

(Macaroni and Chicken Soup)

This soup is a meal in itself and the combination of the pasta, chicken and halloumi cheese makes this soup a real favourite with adults and children alike.

Serves 4 to 6.

6 chicken thighs
1 chicken stock cube
2 litres of water
250g of Greek pasta No. 3 (broken into pieces)
250g of halloumi cheese, grated
salt to taste (if needed)

Put the chicken, stock cube and water into a large saucepan. Bring to the boil; skim off any froth that appears then simmer for 1 hour or until the chicken is very tender. Remove the chicken and set aside. Add the pasta to the stock and cook until tender. Discard the skin and bones from the chicken, pull the meat apart and stir into the soup. Add salt (if needed). Continue to cook until piping hot. Transfer to soup bowls and sprinkle generously with halloumi cheese.

Adam

Michael

The Tasty Greek

WHAT IT TAKES (rugby 2003 final)

I who stand here
Focusing these windows of my eyes
Glazed with honour, purpose, pride and fear
Dreaming, searching for this moment
I prepare my physical strength, my courage, my mind
At this undoubtedly glorious time
To prove I have what it takes to win, like men before me
I cannot falter the slightest degree
Warriors on a battle field
Dissecting the opponent and refusing to yield an inch or two
Will I come up trumps if I see this through?
Can one know if I'm on the winning team?
I ask to myself, can this be fate or an unreachable dream

The Tasty Greek

KOTOPOULO KEH AVGOLEMONO SOOPA

(Chicken and Rice Soup)

This is a popular soup with the Greek communities around the world and is my all time favourite; also this soup is good to eat if feeling unwell. Pay particular attention to the recipe when adding the eggs and lemon juice, because if the soup is too hot the eggs will scramble.

Serves 4 to 6.

4 chicken joints
1 chicken stock cube
2 litres of water
250g of long grain rice
1 teaspoon of salt
3 eggs
juice of 2 lemons

Put the chicken, stock cube and water into a large saucepan. Bring to the boil; skim off any froth that appears then simmer for 1 hour or until the chicken is very tender. Remove the chicken and set aside. Add the rice and salt and simmer until the rice is cooked. Remove from the heat and leave to cool for 10 minutes. Mix the eggs and lemon juice together in a bowl and then add a little of the soup stock to it. Pour into the soup and mix well. Discard the skin and bones from the chicken, pull the meat apart and stir into the soup. Heat the soup until piping hot. Transfer to soup bowls and serve.

Tips
As an alternative turkey can be used instead of chicken.

KREAS SOOPA

(Greek Meat Soup)

This soup is ideal for a cold day. It can be made in advance and heated up in the evening for a very satisfying nutritious meal.

Serves 4 to 6.

600g of stewing steak, cut into chunks
2 litres of water
200g of long grain rice
8 new potatoes, peeled and cut in half
4 carrots, sliced
3 sticks of celery, sliced
1 large courgette (top removed and sliced)
1 chicken or vegetable stock cube
1 teaspoon of salt

Put the steak and water into a large saucepan and bring to the boil. Skim off any froth that appears, then simmer for 30 minutes. Add the rice, potatoes, carrots, celery, courgettes, stock cube and salt. Stir, cover and simmer for a further 30 minutes or until the rice and potatoes are tender.

vegetable

Veggies are best when growing your own,
Out of the garden and into your home,
Add them to your cooking,
And your end up nutritiously healthy looking.

rice

Rice is a starchy seed, which can fill up your tummy,
Added to most things it's really quite yummy,
Use small amounts in cooking cause your find it will grow,
Throw in too much and for sure it'll over flow.

bulg

pasta

wheat

Dried pasta is available wherever you go,
It's made from strong wheat flour and turned into dough -
you know,
It gives us loads of energy when feeling very flat,
My advice is don't eat too much or you'll become
pot bellied and fat.

Combine the harvest when the wheat has grown tall,
Thrash it, crack it, pack it - there's plenty for all,
Add boiling water to re-hydrate the wheat,
Drop in your flavours it makes a nice dish to eat.

KOLOKITHAKI KEH AVGO

(Courgette and Egg)

This dish is one of the simplest of vegetable dishes and can be eaten on its own or with a meat of your choice.

Serves 2.

1 small onion, chopped
3 tablespoons of extra virgin olive oil
4 medium courgettes (tops removed and sliced)
3 eggs, beaten
salt and freshly ground black pepper to taste

Fry the onion in the olive oil until soft. Add the courgettes and cook until light to golden brown. Add the eggs, stir and cook until set, then sprinkle with salt and pepper to taste.

SPANAKI MEH AVGO

(Spinach with Egg)

I would like to think that we all know how good spinach is for us, but sometimes we do not like to eat it on it's own so below is a nice, tasty and simple dish.

Serves 2.

225g of fresh spinach
2 tablespoons of extra virgin olive oil
4 eggs, beaten
salt and freshly ground black pepper to taste

Fry the spinach in the olive oil until wilted. Add the eggs, stir and cook until set, then sprinkle with salt and pepper to taste.

LUVI

(Black Eyed Beans)

The black-eyed bean is very much underused but I find they have a sweeter flavour and cook much quicker than many of the other dried beans. When cooking the beans the water will become discoloured - this is natural, it's the black eye of the bean leaking. Remember to change the water before adding the other ingredients.

<u>Serves 4.</u>

250g of dried black eyed beans
half a tablespoon of salt
1 medium onion, sliced
1 small marrow (remove top, tail and seeds, peel any blemishes and cut into small chunks)
<u>**garnish**</u>
juice of 1 lemon
6 tablespoons of extra virgin olive oil

Cook the beans as directed on the packet. Drain and add fresh water to cover the beans by 2 cm (1 inch). Bring back to the boil then add the salt, onion and marrow. Stir and simmer for a further 30 minutes. Drain off <u>three-quarters</u> of the water. Place into a large serving dish and pour over the lemon juice and olive oil to garnish.

<u>Tips</u>
Alternatively, spinach can be used but must be added 10 minutes before the end of cooking. This is because spinach cooks down quicker than the marrow.

BAMYES YAHNI

(Okra with Potatoes)

Okra is sometimes known as *lady's fingers* and strangely neglected in cooking; it could be something to do with their high price. Best time to use this pod vegetable is while it is still fresh as when they get older they become rubbery and when cooked are sticky.

Serves 4.

12 new potatoes, peeled
5 tablespoons of sunflower oil
500g of fresh okra, tops removed
1 large onion, chopped
2 cloves of garlic, sliced
500g of fresh tomatoes, peeled and chopped **or** 400g tin of tomatoes, chopped
half a tablespoon of salt
550 ml of water

Fry the potatoes in the sunflower oil until golden, remove and arrange in large saucepan. Fry the okra until slightly wilted, remove and arrange over the potatoes. Fry the onion and garlic until just soft, then add the tomatoes, salt and water. Bring to the boil then pour the sauce over the potatoes and okra. Simmer gently for about 1 hour or until the potatoes are tender.

  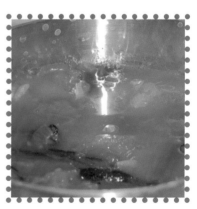

KOUNES KOUCHA MEH LAHANIKA

(Broad Beans with Leaf Beet)

Broad beans are hugely underused but are at the top of the list as nutrition providers as they contain very high levels of protein. It is a good idea to ventilate the kitchen when cooking broad beans as they let off an unusual smell.

Serves 4.

250g of dried split broad beans
1 teaspoon of salt
1 bunch of leaf beet, shredded
2 medium courgettes, top removed and sliced
juice of half a lemon
4 tablespoons of extra virgin olive oil

Cook the beans as directed on the packet. Drain and add fresh water to cover the beans by 2 cm (1 inch). Bring back to the boil, then add the salt, leaf beet and courgettes. Simmer gently for 30 minutes and then drain off all the water. Place into a large serving dish and pour over the lemon juice and olive oil.

BEHIND THE SCENE -z

Building up a picture to show at the cinemas
Pass me the props, lights, reflectors and cameras
Actors in focus – rehearse and speak the lines
Enter set too late – your part is out of time
Got too many shadows, lights need adjusting, adjust their
fixtures
Where are the extras?
Boom-mike held with aching arms above one's head
To hear all that's being said
Duck tape in place to mark a spot
No - move it again, now that's spot-on, stop
Let's move this partition
All who are needed get into position
Nerves arising from deep down in my gut
Not sure I like it – I insist this scene's – CUT!
Running behind now - are we keeping in Max Budget?
that's a real concern
That's it now – lets have it – get ready – ACTION!
This scripted is fantastic lets compliment Dan
With its witty humour and moments of fun, I'm starting to
become a __number 1__ fan
Its not easy keeping all – focused and keen
Who said it was easy working __BEHIND THE SCENE__ -z

The Tasty Greek

FASOLIA STO FOORNOS

(Butter Bean Casserole)

Another delicious dish for vegetarians and meat eaters alike. To take the hassle out of using dried butter beans, two 400g tins can be used instead but remember to give them a good rinse in cold water before adding them to the saucepan.

Serves 4.

250g of dried butter beans (cooked as directed on the packet)
1 litre of water
2 large carrots, sliced
2 sticks of celery, sliced
1 large onion, sliced
500g of fresh tomatoes, peeled and chopped **or** 400g tin of tomatoes, chopped
1 tablespoon of tomato purée
3 tablespoons of fresh flat leaf parsley, chopped
half a teaspoon of black pepper
1 large pinch of ground cinnamon
half a tablespoon of salt
4 tablespoons of extra virgin olive oil
1 tablespoon of lemon juice

Place all the ingredients into a large saucepan and bring to the boil. Reduce the heat and simmer for 5 minutes. Pour into a large casserole dish, cover and cook in a preheated oven on a moderate hot heat for 1 hour. Remove the lid and continue to cook until some of the juice has evaporated.

DOMATES PATATES

(Tomato Flavoured Roast Potatoes)

A flavourful way to enjoy roast potatoes. For a different flavour use garlic salt instead of plain salt to season.

Serves 4 to 6.

small amount of sunflower oil for roasting
12 large potatoes, peeled and cut in half
salt and freshly ground black pepper
1 heaped tablespoon of tomato purée
100 ml of water

Pour the sunflower oil into a large ovenproof dish and heat in a preheated oven until hot (takes about 15 minutes). Remove and then add the potatoes, carefully turning to coat in the hot oil. Season with salt and pepper and return to the oven. Cook for about 1 hour or until the potatoes are cooked through, and then carefully pour off the oil. Mix the tomato purée in the water and pour over the potatoes. Return to the oven for a further 10 minutes.

KOKKINISTO PATATES

(Red Potatoes)

The combination of these ingredients my sound strange but I think whoever makes this recipe will be pleasantly surprised at just how good the potatoes taste.

Serves 4 to 6.

1 kg of new potatoes, peeled and cut half way through
sunflower oil for shallow frying
150 ml dry red wine
1 tablespoon of coriander seeds, lightly crushed

In a large saucepan cook the potatoes in the sunflower oil until cooked through and golden brown. Carefully drain off the excess oil. Add the wine and coriander seeds, stir and bring to the boil and cook rapidly over a high heat until the wine has evaporated.

Tips
Using the above method cooking baby colocassi (*bullez*) with potatoes or on their own make a delicious dish too.

BARAYEMISTES

(Stuffed Vegetables)

This recipe may seem fiddly and time consuming but it's well worth the effort as the end result is very colourful and quite delicious. It just goes to prove we don't only stuff vine leaves. In this recipe I have stuffed the vegetables that I like most but if you prefer to use other vegetables then do so. Remember the rice expands so do not overfill the cavities.

Serves 4 to 6.

stuffing mixture
500g of lean mince pork, lamb or beef
150g of long grain easy cook rice
1 large onion, finely chopped
60g of fresh flat leaf parsley, finely chopped
1 tablespoon of dried mint
500g of fresh tomatoes, peeled and finely chopped **or** 400g tin of tomatoes, finely chopped
1 tablespoon of tomato purée
1 teaspoon of ground cinnamon
half a teaspoon of ground black pepper
half a tablespoon of salt
juice of 1 small lemon
vegetables
4 beefsteak tomatoes
4 small bell peppers
2 medium courgettes
2 small aubergines
for pouring over
200 ml of water
4 tablespoons of extra virgin olive oil

Mix all the ingredients for the *stuffing mixture* together in a large bowl, cover and refrigerate while preparing the vegetables.

Slice the tops off and put to one side. Hollow the middles out of the vegetables <u>taking care not to split the outsides</u>. Reserve the insides of the tomatoes, courgettes and aubergines to make a sauce (<u>see</u> <u>Tips</u>). Stuff the hollowed vegetables with the stuffing mixture and replace the tops. Arrange tightly together in an ovenproof dish then pour in the water and olive oil. Cover and cook in a preheated oven on a moderate hot heat for 1 hour.

<u>Tips</u>

<u>If you would like to make a sauce to go with the vegetables, you will need :-</u>
1 medium onion, chopped
3 tablespoons of extra virgin olive oil
Insides of the vegetables (tomatoes, courgettes, and aubergines) chopped
Salt and freshly ground black pepper to season

<u>Method</u>

In a saucepan soften the onion in the olive oil then add the chopped insides of the vegetables, mix well and simmer for 30 minutes. Put the sauce through a blender and taste. Add seasoning and serve with the above stuffed vegetables or as a sauce for pasta.

The Tasty Greek

KLIFTHARAKI

(Pasta Rice Casserole)

Pasta rice (*Orzo*) is pasta shaped into large grains of rice. This recipe is very tasty, filling and definitely one to cook.

Serves 4.

1 shoulder of lamb, cut into 4 pieces
1 large onion, chopped
500g of fresh tomatoes, peeled and chopped **or** 400g tin of tomatoes, chopped
half a teaspoon of cumin seeds
half a teaspoon of ground cinnamon
half a tablespoon of salt
half a teaspoon of ground black pepper
500 ml of water
250g pasta rice

Place the lamb, onion and tomatoes into a large ovenproof dish. Sprinkle with cumin seeds, cinnamon, salt and pepper, then pour in the water and cover. Cook in a preheated oven on a low heat for 1 and half-hours. Remove from the oven and spoon off excess fat. Stir in the pasta rice. Cover and return to the oven and cook on a moderate heat for a further 15 minutes or until the pasta rice is cooked.

Tips
If you have difficult buying a sliced shoulder of lamb from a supermarket, buy bone-less. Alternatively, a local butcher is the place to go.

MAKARONIA STO FOORNOS

(Macaroni Pasta Dish)

This dish is known as *pastitso* in Greece and to other Greek communities around the world but not in Cyprus, where it is called *makaronia*. I strongly recommend you try this dish because it is absolutely delicious in smell and taste. The Greek pasta number 3 is widely available in supermarkets and Mediterranean food shops.

Serves 6 to 8.

pasta
3 litres of water
1 chicken stock cube
500g of Greek pasta No 3
3 tablespoons of halloumi cheese (taken from the cheese for the sauce)
1 egg white (taken from one egg for the sauce)

mince mixture
1 medium onion, chopped
3 tablespoons of extra virgin olive oil (plus extra for greasing)
750g of lean mince beef
1 large ripe tomato, chopped
45g of fresh flat leaf parsley, chopped
45g of fresh mint, chopped
1 teaspoon of ground cinnamon
1 teaspoon of salt
half a teaspoon of ground black pepper

cheese sauce
100g of plain flour
1 1/4 litres of whole milk (2 pints)
3 eggs, beaten
250g of halloumi cheese, grated
1 tablespoon of dried mint, crushed

pasta- Bring the water to the boil in a large saucepan. Stir in the stock cube and then add the pasta and cook until tender.

Drain and mix in the 3 tablespoons of halloumi cheese and the egg white. Arrange half of the pasta into a large greased ovenproof dish and set aside.

mince mixture- In another saucepan fry the onion in the olive oil until soft, then add the mince beef, mix well and cook until browned. Add the tomato, parsley, mint, cinnamon, salt and pepper, stir and cook for 5 minutes. Pour the mince mixture into the ovenproof dish to cover the pasta.   Cover with the remaining pasta and set aside while preparing the cheese sauce.

cheese sauce- Put the plain flour into a large saucepan and whisk the milk in slowly to avoid lumps, then add the eggs. Place on a moderate heat and bring to the boil, while whisking constantly until it thickens, then add the halloumi cheese and mint. Reduce the heat and simmer gently for 5 minutes. Pour the cheese sauce over the pasta and bake in a preheated oven on a moderate hot heat for about 45 minutes or until dark golden brown.

RISI PILAVI

(Greek Rice)

This tasty rice meal is very simple to make and ideal for barbecues. Remember to keep stirring when adding the vermicelli nest so as not to burn it. Easy cook rice takes about 15 to 20 minutes to cook until tender.

Serves 4 to 6.

1 medium onion, sliced
5 tablespoons of extra virgin olive oil
2 vermicelli nests, broken into pieces
1 level teaspoon of cumin seeds
250g of long grain easy cook rice
1 litre of water
1 chicken or vegetable stock cube
1 teaspoon of salt

In a large saucepan fry the onion in the olive oil until soft, add the vermicelli and cumin seeds, stir and cook until lightly tanned. Add the rice, mix well then cook for a further 1 minute. Stir in the water, stock cube and salt. Bring to the boil, then simmer. Apply the lid on a tilt then cook until the rice is tender. Remove from the heat, cover with a tea towel and replace the lid on a tilt and leave for 30 minutes. Mix well before serving.

Tips
If difficulty in purchasing vermicelli nest, 75g of filini can be used instead.

FAKI, RISI KEH SPANAKI

(Green Lentils, Rice and Spinach)

This recipe is ideal for those cold evenings, as it is warming, filling and nutritious.

<u>Serves 4.</u>

250g of dried green lentils
1 1/4 litres of water
150g of long grain rice
1 teaspoon of salt
2 tablespoons of lemon juice
1 chicken or vegetable stock cube
225g of fresh spinach
1 medium onion, sliced
4 tablespoons of extra virgin olive oil
500g of fresh tomatoes, peeled and chopped <u>or</u> 400g tin of tomatoes, chopped

Cook the lentils as directed on the packet. Drain and return to the saucepan, stir in the water, rice, salt, lemon juice, stock cube and spinach. Bring to the boil and reduce the heat to simmer gently. Meanwhile, in another saucepan fry the onion in the olive oil until soft, add the tomatoes and cook for 5 minutes, then add to the lentils and stir well. Simmer for a further 20 minutes or until the rice is cooked.

<u>Tips</u>
This dish can also be made without the rice.

KREAS MEH RISI KOUPEPIA

(Stuffed Vine Leaves with Meat and Rice)

Stuffed vine leaves are one of the most well known Greek dishes. In Greece they are called *Dolmathes* and many different fillings are used. The vine leaves are fragile when wet - take care not to split them. If using fresh vine leaves they must be young and tender but older tougher leaves are ideal for covering the bottom of the saucepan.

Makes 50.

60 vine leaves
200g of long grain easy cook rice
500g of fresh tomatoes, peeled and finely chopped **or** 400g tin of tomatoes,
finely chopped
60g of fresh mint, finely chopped
60g of fresh flat leaf parsley, finely chopped
half a tablespoon of salt
half a teaspoon of ground black pepper
1 teaspoon of ground cinnamon
3 tablespoons of extra virgin olive oil
juice of half a small lemon
1 small onion, finely chopped
500g of lean mince pork, lamb or beef
1 teaspoon of tomato puree mixed with 200 ml of water
(plus extra water to cover)

Wash the vine leaves in warm water and set aside to drain. Mix all the other ingredients together (apart from extra water to cover) in a large bowl, cover and refrigerate for 1 hour. Lay a vine leaf out flat with the dull/under side facing up. Put a heaped tablespoon of the mixture in the centre, fold the side's inward and roll it up into a cigar shape. Repeat this until 50 are made. Line the bottom of a saucepan with 5 vine leaves. Pack the 50 stuffed vine leaves (koupepia) tightly in layers into the saucepan.

Cover with the remaining vine leaves then pour in enough water to cover by 2 cm (1 inch). Put a tea plate on top of them and place a small weight **or** a teacup full of water on top of the tea plate for a weight. Bring to the boil, then simmer gently for 40 minutes or until the rice is cooked.

The Tasty Greek

POURGOURI KOUPEPIA

(Bulgar wheat stuffed Vine Leaves)

This is a vegetarian version of stuffed vine leaves. Do not roll too tightly as the bulgar wheat will expand while cooking and split the leaves.

Makes 50.

60 vine leaves
500g of bulgar wheat (large coarse grain)
500g of fresh tomatoes, peeled and finely chopped or 400g tin
of tomatoes, finely chopped
45g of fresh flat leaf parsley, finely chopped
1 tablespoon of dried mint, crushed
half a tablespoon of salt
half a teaspoon of ground black pepper
half a teaspoon of ground cinnamon
juice of half a small lemon
75 ml of extra virgin olive oil
1 medium onion, finely chopped
150 ml of water (plus extra water to cover)

Wash the vine leaves in warm water and set aside to drain. Mix all the other ingredients together (apart from extra water to cover) in a large bowl. Lay a vine leaf out flat with the dull/under side facing up. Put a heaped tablespoon of the mixture in the centre, fold the side's inward and roll it up into a cigar shape. Repeat this until 50 are made. Line the bottom of a large saucepan with 5 vine leaves. Pack the 50 stuffed vine leaves (koupepia) tightly in layers into the saucepan. Cover with the remaining vine leaves then pour in enough water to cover by 2 cm (1 inch). Put a tea plate on top of them and place a small weight **or** a teacup full of water on top of the tea plate for a weight. Bring to the boil, then simmer gently until the water has been absorbed or the bulgar wheat is cooked.

POURGOURI PILAVI

(Bulgar Wheat Dish)

This recipe can be made using cous-cous if preferred. If using boiling water from a kettle, I recommend you take the saucepan of the heat before adding the water and allow the temperature to drop a little before placing back over a low heat to simmer for the 5 minutes.

Serves 4 to 6.

**1 large onion, thinly sliced
5 tablespoons of extra virgin olive oil <u>or</u> sunflower oil
4 vermicelli nests, broken into pieces
250g of bulgar wheat
2 medium tomatoes, finely chopped (optional)
1 litre of water
1 teaspoon of salt**

In a large saucepan fry the onion in the oil until soft, add the vermicelli, bulgar wheat and tomatoes (if using), stir to avoid sticking and cook for 1 minute. Add the water and salt, mix well and bring to the boil, then simmer for 5 minutes. Take off the heat and cover with a tea towel for 20 minutes. Mix well and served with plain Greek yogurt and black olives.

Tips
Flavours of your choice can be added to this dish, for instance - chopped herbs or chopped olives, cucumber, peppers, etc. Either, gently mix them in with a fork just before you cover with a tea towel or when completely cold.

If difficulty in purchasing vermicelli nest, 75g of filini can be used instead.

fish

The sea is vast and fish stocks should be plenty,
Leave trawler nets in too long in time the sea will be empty,
Fresh fish is not when its eye is dull and like jelly,
If it does not taste like the sea chuck it it's smelly.

pork

Most pork meat is fine grained, pale pink, moist and tender,
Unlike red meat its taste is easy to remember,
Mild on the pallet it goes down well,
Whether grilling, frying, baking or barbecuing - yum yum
delicious what a lovely smell.

beef

Beef is best when the meat is of prime quality and young,
To tenderise to a plum red colour and slightly moist means
it has been properly hung,
Some beef seem sinewy, fleckled and tough looking,
Such cuts improve with flavour and tenderness when slow
cooking.

poultry

The best tasting chicken is when allowed to run free,
Open up those barn doors and leave these birds be,
Lean is this white meat and a light taste on the pallet,
Can you believe it?
Nowadays you can roast one still in its packet.

lamb

Lamb is tender meat, light red in colour,
Distinctive is its aroma and delicious in flavour,
Where as mutton is old sheep much tougher and stronger
in taste,
Cook the traditional kleftiko - I know you will want more and
leave nothing to waste.

game

Wild animals and birds which are hunted and eaten,
Some countries have a close season - so hunting is forbidden,
Free to run around this meat can be too tough and hard to chew,
Then I suggest you braise it or cook up a stew.

PSARI STO FOORNOS

(Marinated Grey Mullet)

This fish is much underused and it has a bad reputation for being a sea bottom feeder. Marinating the fish in lemon and salt over night helps to clean it thoroughly and bring out the flavour. When cooked this way it makes a very nice dish to eat.

Serves 2.

2 large grey mullet
2 tablespoons of salt
juice of 2 lemons
half a teaspoon of ground black pepper
2 bay leaves
4 spring onions, chopped
extra virgin olive oil to drizzle
60 ml of water

Clean, scale and wash the fish and put into a large dish. Sprinkle all over with the salt and lemon juice, cover and leave over night in the refrigerator. Place the fish in an ovenproof dish and sprinkle with pepper; place a bay leaf and the spring onions on top of each fish. Drizzle with olive oil and pour the water in the dish. Cover with foil and cook in a preheated oven on a moderate heat for about 30 minutes or until the fish is cooked through.

Tips
Fishmongers will usually clean whole fish ready for cooking.

PSARI DIARNIKO

(Fried Red Snapper)

Its recommended you ask the fishmonger to clean, remove the vein, the fins, scales and head as this fish is very bony and difficult to cut through and the fins have needle like spikes, unless you have some experience in doing the job yourself. Nevertheless, a nice simple recipe to bring out the full delicate flavour of the red snapper.

Serves 2.

2 small to medium red snappers
2 lemons, cut into quarters (plus extra for serving)
1 tablespoon of salt
4 tablespoons of plain flour
sunflower oil for shallow frying

Clean, scale and wash the fish, pat dry with absorbent paper and score the skin three times on each side. Place the fish into a large bowl. Rub and squeeze the lemon quarters all over the fish then gently rub in the salt on both sides and inside the cavity. Cover and refrigerate for 1 hour. Drain and dust with the plain flour. Fry the fish in the sunflower oil over a moderate heat until cooked through. Serve with lemon quarters.

GARITHES KEH FETA

(Prawns and Feta)

This might seem an unusual combination but its quick to make, healthy and a very delicious meal. When served the meal looks beautiful with its red, pink and white colours.

Serves 2.

4 small shallots, finely chopped
1 clove of garlic, crushed
2 tablespoons of extra virgin olive oil
500g of fresh tomatoes, peeled and finely chopped **or** 400g tin of tomatoes, finely chopped
1 tablespoon of tomato purée
1 heaped tablespoon of fresh flat leaf parsley, finely chopped
200g of raw tiger prawns (cleaned and veins removed)
100g of feta cheese, cubed
salt and fleshly ground black pepper to taste

In a saucepan fry the shallots and garlic in the olive oil until soft. Add the tomatoes, tomato purée and flat leaf parsley then cook for 5 minutes. Add the prawns and continue to cook until they turn pink in colour. Take of the heat and stir in the feta cheese, then add salt and pepper to taste. Serve this dish with plain boiled rice and lemon wedges.

PSARI LEMONATO DIARNIKO

(Sprat Fish)

These lovely little creamy crispy fish are delicious as a starter or as part of a traditional Greek mezethes.

Serves 2 to 4.

500g of sprat fish (gut, but leave fish whole)
juice of 2 lemons (plus lemon wedges to serve)
half a tablespoon of salt
plain flour (for rolling the fish in)
sunflower oil for shallow frying

Wash the fish well, drain and place in a large bowl. Pour the lemon juice and salt over the fish and mix well. Cover and refrigerate for 30 minutes. Drain off the liquid and roll the fish in the flour. Fry for about 5 minutes on each side or until golden brown and crispy. Drain on absorbent paper and transfer to a serving plate with lemon wedges.

Tips
The season for this small silvery–skinned fish is October to March.

SIPKTHES MEH KRASI

(Cuttlefish with Red Wine)

Although larger than the squid family it is related. Take care while cooking the cuttlefish in the hot oil, as it tends to spit. Nowadays, the cuttlefish are sold without their ink sack; they are removed and sold in good delicatessens. When the ink is cooked with the cuttlefish it produces a nice peppery flavour.

Serves 4.

1 kg of cuttlefish, cleaned (cut into thick strips and leave tentacles whole)
juice of 1 lemon
1 tablespoon of salt
80 ml of sunflower oil
80 ml of malt vinegar
150 ml of dry red wine
2 bay leaves
2 cm piece of cinnamon stick (1 inch)
salt and freshly ground black pepper to season

Place the cuttlefish in a large bowl. Add the lemon juice and salt, mix well, cover and refrigerate for 1 hour. Wash the cuttlefish and pat dry with absorbent paper. Pour half the sunflower oil (40-ml) into a large saucepan and heat until very hot. Carefully add the cuttlefish and malt vinegar, stir and cook for about 10 minutes or until all the water has come out of the cuttlefish. Drain well and return to the saucepan with the remaining sunflower oil. Add the red wine, bay leaves, cinnamon stick, salt and pepper. Bring to the boil, then simmer for a further 25 minutes or until the red wine has evaporated. Drain away the oil and serve.

KALAMARI DIARNIKO

(Fried Squid)

Ready prepared squid tubes can be purchased to save time on cleaning them. Take care while cooking the squid in the hot oil, as it tends to spit. When cooked it should look slightly golden and pinkish in colour, tender and taste like the sea. Cook them too long and they will end up rubbery.

Serves 2 to 4.

sunflower oil for shallow frying
1 kg of squid, cleaned and chopped or sliced into rings
1 lemon, cut into wedges
salt to taste

Heat the sunflower oil in a saucepan then carefully add the squid in batches and fry for 5 minutes. Remove with a slotted spoon and drain on absorbent paper. Transfer to a serving plate with the lemon wedges. Add salt to taste.

Tips
For a crunchier texture dip the squid into seasoned flour and fry in a non-stick frying pan.

PSARI SOUVLAKIA

(Barbecue Fish)

Care is needed when preparing the fish and cooking it this way makes a deliciously different dish and takes less time to cook than the meat souvlakia.

Serves 4 to 6.

1.5 kg of small fish, whole **or** fillets of firm textured fish
extra virgin olive oil for brushing
salt and freshly ground black pepper to season
3 lemons, quartered

Clean, scale and wash the fish and pat dry with absorbent paper. Score the skin of the whole fish only. Brush over with the olive oil and season with salt and pepper. Place the fish in a barbecue fish holder. Cook over a hot barbecue, turning regularly until the fish is cooked through. Serve with the lemon quarters.

Tips
To add flavour to the fish use - 100 ml of extra virgin olive oil, 1 tablespoon of fresh flat leaf parsley (finely chopped) 1 tablespoon of lemon juice and a pinch of salt. Mix all the ingredients together in a bowl and brush onto the fish just before cooking.

KOTOPOULO STO FOORNOS

(Roast Chicken)

Putting cinnamon on chicken gives it a beautiful aromatic smell and taste. To check if the chicken is cooked through cut between the breast and thigh, if the flesh is pink the chicken needs more time in the oven. When washing the chicken I trim and remove the parson's nose, the end part of the wings and any spare fat around the bottom end.

Serves 4 to 6.

1 whole chicken (cleaned and ready for roasting)
1 teaspoon of ground cinnamon
salt and freshly ground black pepper to season

Wash the chicken and place into a roasting tray. Sprinkle with the cinnamon and season with salt and pepper. Cook uncovered in a preheated oven on a moderate hot heat until the chicken has cooked through and the skin is crispy. Rest the chicken for 10 minutes in a warm place before cutting and serving.

Tips
If preferred, a stuffing mixture of your choice can be added before cooking.

KOTOPOULO TAVAN

(Chicken Tavan)

This is a favoured dish by most Greeks - with its deep red colour, delicious taste and is very simple to make.

<u>Serves 4.</u>

8 chicken joints
1 kg of new potatoes, peeled and left whole
2 medium onions, sliced
1 teaspoon of salt
half a teaspoon of ground black pepper
1 teaspoon of ground cinnamon
2 tablespoons of extra virgin olive oil
500g of fresh tomatoes, peeled and chopped **or** 400g tin of tomatoes, chopped
1 tablespoon of tomato purée
500 ml of water

Mix all the ingredients together in large ovenproof dish and cover. Cook in a preheated oven on a moderate low heat for 2 hours.

<u>Tips</u>
Traditionally this dish is cooked in earthenware cooking pots.

COLOCASSI MEH HIRINO

(Colocassi with Pork)

Colocassi is a very unusual root vegetable. When whole and not peeled it is a muddy looking tuber but when washed and peeled it is creamy white in colour. I have purposely left out the measured amount of water used for this recipe as colocassi come in many different sizes. Although using a large colocassi the amount of water needed may vary.

Serves 4 to 6.

750g of belly pork strips, remove rind and cut into 5 cm pieces (2 inches)
4 tablespoons of sunflower oil
2 medium onions, chopped
1 large colocassi, peeled and chopped into large chunks
3 sticks of celery, sliced
2 heaped tablespoons of tomato purée
enough water to cover
1 teaspoon of salt
juice of 1 small lemon

In a large saucepan fry the pork in the sunflower oil to seal, remove and set aside. Add the onions, stir and cook for 5 minutes. Add the colocassi; mix well then cook for a further 5 minutes. Return the pork to the saucepan then add the celery, tomato purée, enough water to cover by 5 cm (2 inches) and mix well. Bring to the boil then add the salt and 1 teaspoon of the lemon juice. Cover and simmer gently for about 1 hour or until the colocassi has softened. Uncover and add the remaining lemon juice, stir and continue to cook for a further 10 minutes.

Tips
The colocassi can be purchased from a Mediterranean green grocer. This vegetable is also known as *taro*.

HIRINO MEH BIZELIA

(Pork with Peas)

A very simple dish that brings out the best in pork chops. As the pork chops are often very dry, cooking them this way produces a melt in the mouth experience.

Serves 4.

4 large pork chops
5 tablespoons of sunflower oil
2 medium onions, sliced
400 ml of water
500g of fresh or frozen peas
500g of fresh tomatoes, peeled and chopped **or** 400g tin of tomatoes, chopped
1 teaspoon of tomato purée
1 teaspoon of salt

Seal the pork chops in a frying pan with 3 tablespoons of the sunflower oil. Meanwhile, in a large saucepan, fry the onions in the remaining oil for 5 minutes. Stir in the water, peas, tomatoes, tomato purée and salt. Bring to the boil, then simmer for 10 minutes. Add the pork chops to the pea sauce and mix well. Cover and simmer for 50 minutes. Uncover and continue to simmer for a further 10 minutes.

HIRINO MEH BRASENO FASOLIA

(Pork with Green Beans)

This is a lovely filling dish especially if you dip crusty bread to mop up the juice. Runner beans can be used for this meal instead of the green beans and cooked in the same way. Also a chopped clove of garlic can be added at the same time as the onion, try it and see.

Serves 4 to 6.

12 new potatoes, peeled and cut in half
sunflower oil for shallow frying
750g of pork, cut into bite size chunks
1 medium onion, chopped
750g of green beans (tops removed)
1 litre of water
500g of fresh tomatoes, peeled and chopped **or** 400g tin of tomatoes, chopped
juice of half a lemon
1 tablespoon of tomato purée
half a tablespoon of salt

In a large saucepan fry the potatoes in the sunflower oil until golden brown, remove and set aside. Add the meat and cook to seal, remove and set aside. Add the onion and cook for 5 minutes then add the green beans, stir and cook for a further 10 minutes. Drain off excess oil. Stir in the water, tomatoes, lemon juice, tomato purée and salt. Return the potatoes and meat to the saucepan and mix well. Bring to the boil, cover and simmer for 40 minutes. Uncover and continue to cook for a further 10 minutes.

SIKOTAKI AFELIA

(Pork Liver)

Traditionally, this dish contained hearts, lungs and liver. With the meat regulations today, lungs are <u>not</u> used. I have left out hearts due to preference but if desired. 500g of hearts cut into bite size pieces and 500g of liver cut into bite size pieces can be used instead of just the liver. Cooked in the same way as below.

<u>Serves 4 to 6.</u>

1 kg of pig <u>or</u> lambs liver, cut into bite size pieces
juice of 1 lemon
1 teaspoon of salt
80 ml sunflower oil
150 ml of dry red wine
2 tablespoons of coriander seeds, lightly crushed

Wash the liver very well and put into a large saucepan. Add the lemon juice and salt, stir and simmer for 10 minutes. Drain and return to the saucepan. Stir in the sunflower oil, red wine and coriander seeds then continue to cook until the wine has evaporated. Drain off excess oil and serve.

I CAN NOT WAIT FOR YOU FOREVER

I wait and wait
But - who could possibly know how much I frustrate
Tormented - I eager to see your face
My beauty so full of grace
Although - in your eyes
I see too many good-byes
Those windows to one's soul
Frightened - I fear this chapter one-day will close
I wait and wait
Like a fool I call again - again no answer - I guess I'm too late
The messages stack high
But still I get no reply
At times, my life seems motionless
Does my sweetheart ever careless
A heavy sigh reaches my breath
I strongly feel - I will take this anxiety to my death
I wait and wait
Struggle with my emotions - this is what I hate
Dear me - do I really have to beg you?
Can someone tell me - what must I do to get through?
This uncontrollable depression that blinds my mind
I drift through streets - cause its you I search to find
If only my sweetheart knew
My heart churns in my mouth - I chew
I wait and wait
I just wish you'd find the time for us to date
Why do I feel so totally lovesick?
Like an addict who can't wait to get their next fix
I dread when I'm all-alone
It's then I sit patiently staring at the telephone
Heaven knows if and when you'll ever be mine
To take away my sorrow and give me peace of mind

The Tasty Greek

77

SHEFTALIA

(Greek Sausage)

The caul-fat is white in colour and is stringy in a cobweb sort of way when carefully pulled apart. This might seem a strange combination together but the caul-fat is used for wrapping the pork mince, adding moisture and to increase the flavour in the sausages. Once cooked either eat whole or remove the caul-fat immediately before serving.

Serves 4 to 6.

500g of thin caul-fat (fat from around a lamb's belly)
2 tablespoons of lemon juice
meat mixture
500g of lean mince pork
2 medium onions, finely chopped
45g of fresh flat leaf parsley, finely chopped
half a tablespoon of salt
half a teaspoon of ground black pepper
1 large pinch of ground cumin
2 tablespoons of extra virgin olive oil

Wash the caul-fat very well in a small bowl of warm water and the lemon juice. Drain and cut into 16 cm by 13 cm (6 1/2 inch x 5 inch) size pieces and set aside. Mix the meat mixture together in a large bowl. Lay the caul-fat out and put 1 heaped tablespoon of the mixture in the centre, fold the side's inwards and roll up into a sausage shape. Arrange and cook over a hot barbecue turning regularly until the sausages are cooked through (beware, the barbecue will flame when the fat drips onto the hot charcoal). Alternatively, place the sausages in an ovenproof dish in a single layer. Cook in a preheated oven on a moderate hot heat for 20 minutes and then carefully pour off the excess fat. Return to the oven and continue to cook until golden brown.

Tips
Caul-fat can be purchased from most independent butchers.

LOUKANIKA

(Pork and Wine Sausages)

These sausages are very popular in most Greek households and have a unique flavour. The Cyprus authentic ready-made shop variety have dried dark reddish-black fragrant berries added known as (*Shin-yon*) but not easy to buy and I have left them out of the recipe for this reason. Pack the sausage filling tightly into the skin as shrinking can occur when draining.

Makes 8 sausages.

filling
1 kg of lean mince pork
500 ml of dry red wine
1 tablespoon of salt
1 heaped tablespoon of coriander seeds, lightly crushed
skin
1 four metre length of pork sausage skin
50 ml of dry red wine

Combine all the ingredients for the filling in a large bowl, mix well and cover. Wash the sausage skin very well and soak in the 50-ml of wine and cover. Put both the sausage filling and the skin in the fridge for 2 days.

Method 1 (requires two people)

Wash the sausage skin before use. Using a large disposable-piping bag, pipe the entire filling into the sausage skin, while carefully pushing the filling down, and then tie a knot at the piped end. Lay the long sausage out onto a clean surface and twist to make the required sausage lengths and then tie a knot at the other end. Take the length of unfilled skin and tie it around the twists in the sausages. Pierce the skin all over using a cocktail stick. Hang the sausages up in a cool dry place over a bowl to drain for 3 days.

Can be grilled, baked or barbecued.

Method 2 (requires one person)

Wash the sausage skin before use. Cut the sausage skin into 4 equal lengths. Tie a knot in the middle of each length. Using your hands open the skin and push the filling carefully in. Pack the filling tight into the skin to the required length (Approx. 15 cm/6 inches long). Repeat this until the entire filling is used up and then secure each sausage with a knot. Pierce the skin all over using a cocktail stick. Hang the sausages up in a cool dry place over a bowl to drain for 3 days. Can be grilled, baked or barbecued. (Using this method, there will be some sausage skin waste).

Tips
Sausage skins can be purchased from most independent butchers. Order in advance. Preserve any excess sausage skins in plenty of salt and store in a dry cool place.

smoke flavoured
If a smoked flavour is preferred, using a barbecue light a hand full of charcoal, let it burn red in colour (very hot), then add some fine or coarse saw-dust, hang the loukanika sausages in the smoke for 2 hours.
Caution: If smoking the sausages in an enclosed area beware of the fire risk.

ARNI KEH DOMATES KLEFTIKO

(Lamb and Tomato Parcels)

Delicious! Cooking lamb this way I have never tasted it so good and then the potatoes that have been cooked using the lamb juices - well it just tantalises the taste buds.

Serves 4.

1 shoulder of lamb, cut into 4 pieces
salt and freshly ground black pepper to season
4 large pinches of cumin seeds
2 medium tomatoes
4 bay leaves
120 ml of water
8 medium potatoes, peeled and cut in half

Take 4 pieces of cooking foil, large enough to hold the lamb. Place the lamb in the centre of each piece of foil and sprinkle with salt, pepper and cumin seeds. Slice each tomato into 4 pieces and put 2 pieces and a bay leaf on top of each piece of lamb. Bring the foil edges up and pour 30 ml (2 tbsp.) of water into each lamb parcel. Wrap them up carefully to seal. Place the lamb parcels into an ovenproof dish and cook in a preheated oven on a moderate heat for 1 hour. Place the potatoes under the lamb parcels and pierce the bottom of the foil to let the juices run over the potatoes. Return to the oven and cook until the potatoes are tender.

Tips
If you have difficulty buying a sliced shoulder of lamb from a supermarket, buy boneless. Alternatively, a local butcher is the place to go.

ARNI MEH PATATES KOKKINISTO
(Lamb with Potatoes in Wine)

This is an all in one meat melting and colourful dish with plenty of flavour.

Serves 4 to 6.

10 medium potatoes, peeled and cut in half
1 shoulder of lamb, cut into 4 to 6 pieces
400 ml of dry red wine
4 tablespoons of sunflower oil
1 teaspoon of salt
2 tablespoons of lemon juice
200 ml of passata
1 litre of water

Marinate the potatoes and lamb in the wine for 30 minutes. In a large saucepan fry the potatoes in the sunflower oil until lightly browned, remove and set aside. Fry the meat to seal then return the potatoes. Add 200-ml of the wine, salt, lemon juice, passata and water. Mix well, cover and simmer gently for 1 and half hours.

KLEFTIKO

(Traditional Mutton Roast)

Kleftiko, meaning theft, refers to an old tale when livestock was taken and cooked on the run. This is a lovely way to cook mutton (name given to old sheep meat) which needs long slow cooking to bring out its delicious flavour. The best place to buy mutton is at independent butchers, as supermarkets do not stock it.

Serves 6.

6 pieces of mutton (shoulder or leg)
salt and freshly ground black pepper to season
6 large pinches of cumin seeds
6 bay leaves
180 ml of water

Take 6 pieces of cooking foil large enough to hold the mutton. Place the mutton in the centre of each foil then sprinkle with salt, pepper, cumin seeds and place a bay leaf on top. Bring the foil edges up and pour 30 ml (2 tbsp.) of water into each mutton parcel. Wrap them up carefully to seal. Place the mutton parcels in an earthenware dish and cook in a preheated oven on a low heat for 3 hours or until the meat is very tender.

Tips
This dish is best served with the delicious tomato flavoured roast potatoes.

KOUBEZ

(Cous-Cous and Minced Lamb Sausage)

Using boiling water from a kettle is a quick method for this recipe, but check to see how much water the kettle holds first and always be careful when using boiling water because of scolding. Adding the plain flour to the cous-cous helps to bond and keep the sausages in shape before frying; it also helps to give them a crispy texture when cooked.

Serves 4 to 6.

wheat mixture
500g of fine cous-cous
1 teaspoon of salt
1 1/2 litres of boiling water
2 heaped tablespoons of plain flour
filling mixture
3 medium onions, finely chopped
3 tablespoons of sunflower oil (plus extra oil for deep-frying)
350g of lean mince lamb
1 teaspoon of salt
half a teaspoon of ground black pepper
half a teaspoon of ground cinnamon
40g of fresh flat leaf parsley, finely chopped
2 lemons, cut into wedges to serve

Place the cous-cous into a large bowl. Add the salt then carefully pour in boiling water. Mix well, cover with a tea towel and set aside for about 2 hours to allow the liquid to absorb and cous-cous to go cold. Fry the onions in the sunflower oil until soft, then add the mince lamb, salt, pepper, cinnamon and parsley, mix well. Cook for 20 minutes on a low heat then pour into a sieve. Set aside to drain and to let the filling mixture go cold.

Mix the flour into the cous-cous and knead for 5 minutes, cover and set aside to stand for 30 minutes.

With wet hands take a handful of the *wheat mixture*. Roll and squeeze into a fat sausage shape and carefully push your thumb in at one end to create a cavity. Put a tablespoon of the *filling mixture* in then shape it into a rugby ball shape. Leave uncovered to rest for 10 minutes. Deep-fry them in batches until golden brown. Drain on absorbent paper and transfer to a serving dish with the lemon wedges.

ARNI SKORTHO KEH LEMONI PATATES

(Lamb and Lemony Potato Roast)

Cooking and eating lamb is one of my favourite past times, especially when combined with garlic and lemon thyme, cooked until brown and crispy then served with the delicious potatoes, add to that seasonal vegetables, could you really want anything more for a Sunday lunch. I find it hard putting a time on cooking a leg of lamb due to its size, as I like mine to be cooked through, I check the lamb after one and half hours first then every fifteen minutes there after until the juices run clear.

Serves 4 to 6.

lamb
1 leg of lamb
2 cloves of garlic, cut into 10 slices
10 small sprigs (pieces) of fresh lemon thyme
salt and freshly ground black pepper to season
potatoes
10 large potatoes, peeled and cut in half
lemon sauce
juice of 1 small lemon
5 tablespoons of extra virgin olive oil
1 heaped tablespoon of lemon thyme leaves, chopped
1 teaspoon of salt
pinch of ground black pepper

lamb- Wash the leg of lamb, trim off excess fat and place into a roasting tray. Make 10 incisions with a sharp knife then push a piece of garlic and lemon thyme in each incision. Sprinkle with the salt and pepper, cover with foil and place in a preheated hot oven for 15 minutes. Turn the oven down to a moderate hot heat and cook until the juices run clear when pierced with a skewer. Remove the foil and continue to cook until the meat is nicely browned. Rest the lamb for 10 minutes in a warm place before carving.

potatoes- Place the potatoes in a saucepan of hot water and simmer for 10 minutes. Meanwhile, combine all the ingredients for the *lemon sauce* in a jug and mix well. Drain the potatoes and place in a roasting tray. Pour the lemon sauce over the potatoes and roll them around until covered. Cook in the oven with the lamb until golden brown and crispy.

KREAS SOUVLAKIA

(Meat Kebabs)

Souvlakia is the Greek word for *skewer* or *spit* and refers to the way the meat is cooked. A steak is usually a slice of a good cut of meat. Using meat steaks is the easiest and simplest way for a souvlaki barbecue, although, I've used a leg of lamb and shoulder of pork before which I have cut up myself but its all down to personal choice and taste. Meat with a little fat in it can provide more flavour. If using wooden skewers they must be soaked in water before use. This will prevent them from burning. Never mind the weather - get that barbecue out and enjoy.

Serves 6.

500g of lamb steaks
500g of pork steaks
4 chicken breast
1 turkey breast
salt to season
3 lemons, quartered

Cut the meat into 2 to 5 cm chunks (1 to 2 inches). Carefully thread onto skewers and lightly sprinkle with salt. Arrange in a single layer and cook over a hot barbecue turning regularly until the meat is cooked through. Put the cooked meat into a large saucepan, cover and place near the barbecue to keep warm before serving. Serve with the lemon quarters, a bowl of Greek salad, pilavi, pitta bread and tzatziki.

Tips
Alternatively, cook under the grill or in a griddle pan on a moderate heat, turning regularly until the meat is cooked through.

MOUSSAKA

(Tasty Moussaka)

I've heard so many times in the past, chefs say "watch me make this authentic Greek moussaka" and I think to myself who are these people kidding because half the ingredients they use are Italian. Now is your chance to make the best, nutritious and most filling Greek moussaka you have ever come across with the most tastiest cheese sauce ever. I recommend you try it and see.

Serves 6 to 8.

6 medium potatoes, peeled and sliced
2 medium aubergines (remove green top only, cut into round slices
about 1 cm thick)
3 medium courgettes (remove top only, cut into round slices
about 1 cm thick)
sunflower oil for greasing and brushing
mince mixture
1 medium onion, finely chopped
3 tablespoons of sunflower oil
750g of lean mince lamb
2 large ripe tomatoes, finely chopped
2 tablespoons of fresh flat leaf parsley, finely chopped
2 tablespoons of fresh mint, finely chopped
1 teaspoon of salt
half a teaspoon of ground black pepper
1 teaspoon of ground cinnamon
1 teaspoon of tomato purée
80 ml of dry red wine
3 bay leaves
cheese sauce
100g of plain flour
1 1/4 litres of whole milk (2 pints)
2 eggs, beaten

250g of halloumi cheese, grated
1 tablespoon of dried mint, crushed

Place the potato, aubergine and courgette slices in single layer on lightly greased baking trays and brush over with sunflower oil. Cook them in a preheated oven on a moderate heat until lightly browned. Set aside while making the mince mixture.

mince mixture- In a large saucepan fry the onion in the 3 tablespoons of sunflower oil until soft. Add the mince lamb and cook until browned then drain of excess oil. Add the tomatoes, parsley, mint, salt, pepper, cinnamon, tomato purée, red wine, and the bay leaves, mix well and simmer for 10 minutes. Grease a large ovenproof dish with sunflower oil. Arrange half of the potatoes, aubergines and courgettes in layers. Top with half of the mince mixture then arrange the remaining potatoes, aubergines and courgettes on top. Pour over the rest of the mince mixture and set aside while making the cheese sauce.

cheese sauce- Put the plain flour into a large saucepan and whisk the milk in slowly to avoid lumps, then add the eggs. Place on a moderate heat and bring to the boil, while whisking constantly until it thickens, then add the halloumi cheese and mint. Reduce the heat and simmer gently for 5 minutes. Pour the cheese sauce over the moussaka and bake in a preheated oven on a moderate hot heat for about 45 minutes or until dark golden brown.

Tips
Alternatively, water can be used instead of dry red wine.

SHISH KOFTI

(Mince Lamb Kebabs)

The best way to remove juice from grated onions is to place into a clean tea towel, bring the corners together, twist and squeeze. Remember to keep an eye on the lamb kebabs when cooking and turn them regularly as the barbecue can flame and burn them.

Makes about 8 to 10.

500g of lean mince lamb
2 large onions, grated and squeezed to remove juice
1 fat clove of garlic, crushed
2 tablespoons of fresh flat leaf parsley, finely chopped
1 teaspoon of ground hot chilli powder
1 egg
salt and freshly ground black pepper to season

Put all the ingredients into a large bowl and squeeze together with your hands for 3 minutes, cover and refrigerate for 30 minutes. Then either, press onto skewers into flat sausage shapes or make into round burger shapes. Arrange in a single layer and cook over a hot barbecue, turning regularly until the meat is browned and cooked through. Alternatively, cook in a lightly greased frying pan or under the grill on a moderate heat. Serve with pitta bread, Greek salad and plain Greek yogurt.

Tips
For a different flavour use 2 tablespoons of freshly chopped mint instead of the flat leaf parsley and leave out the garlic and chilli powder.

KEFTETHES

(Greek Meat Balls)

Most of the ingredients used in this recipe have to be finely chopped; to make light work of this using a food processor will reduce the preparation time considerably.

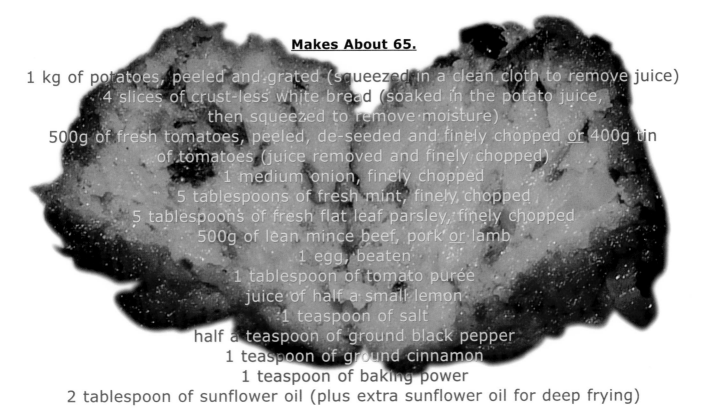

Makes About 65.

1 kg of potatoes, peeled and grated (squeezed in a clean cloth to remove juice)
4 slices of crust-less white bread (soaked in the potato juice, then squeezed to remove moisture)
500g of fresh tomatoes, peeled, de-seeded and finely chopped <u>or</u> 400g tin of tomatoes (juice removed and finely chopped)
1 medium onion, finely chopped
5 tablespoons of fresh mint, finely chopped
5 tablespoons of fresh flat leaf parsley, finely chopped
500g of lean mince beef, pork <u>or</u> lamb
1 egg, beaten
1 tablespoon of tomato purée
juice of half a small lemon
1 teaspoon of salt
half a teaspoon of ground black pepper
1 teaspoon of ground cinnamon
1 teaspoon of baking power
2 tablespoon of sunflower oil (plus extra sunflower oil for deep frying)

Combine all the ingredients together in a large bowl (apart from the sunflower oil for deep-frying) then cover and refrigerate for 30 minutes. Shape the mixture into small golf ball size or small rugby balls and place onto a large tray. Fry in batches in hot oil until dark golden brown. Remove with a slotted spoon and drain on absorbent paper. Transfer to a serving dish and serve hot or cold with pitta bread, Greek salad and plain Greek Yogurt.

VODHINO, KOLOKITHAKI KEH MELITZANA

(Steak, Courgette and Aubergine)

Another favourite of mine, this is so tasty and enjoyable when the steak just melts in your mouth. It's an ideal dish to make for that special someone in your life.

Serves 2.

sunflower oil for greasing, brushing and shallow frying
1 medium aubergine (remove green top only, slice lengthways **or** cut into round slices about 1 cm thick)
2 medium courgettes (remove top only, slice lengthways **or** cut into round slices about 1 cm thick)
600g of rump steak, cut into chunks
1 medium onion, sliced
2 cloves of garlic, diced small
725 ml of water
250 ml of passata **or** 400g tin of tomatoes, chopped
1 tablespoon of tomato purée
1 teaspoon of salt

Place the aubergine and courgette slices in single layer on lightly greased baking trays and brush over with sunflower oil. Cook them in a preheated oven on a moderate heat until lightly browned, then set aside. In a large saucepan fry the steak in sunflower oil to seal, remove with a slotted spoon and arrange in a large ovenproof cooking dish. Arrange the aubergine and courgette slices over the meat and set aside. Fry the onions and garlic until soft then drain off excess oil. Add the water, passata **or** tin tomatoes, tomato purée, and salt. Bring to the boil and pour the sauce over the top of the other ingredients. Cover and cook in a preheated oven on a moderate hot heat for about 1 hour or until the meat is tender.

KOUNILI STIFADO

(Rabbit with Onions)

Cut the rabbit at the joints to avoid splintering the bones. Washing the rabbit with lemon juice helps to clean it.

Serves 2.

juice of 1 lemon
1 rabbit, cleaned and jointed
4 tablespoons of sunflower oil
5 medium onions, sliced
250 ml of water (plus extra water)
500g of fresh tomatoes, peeled and chopped **or** 400g tin of tomatoes, chopped
1 tablespoon of tomato purée
40 ml of malt vinegar
1 chicken stock cube
2 bay leaves
1 teaspoon of salt

Pour the lemon juice into a small bowl of water and wash the rabbit very well, drain and pat dry on absorbent paper. Heat the sunflower oil in a large saucepan until very hot. Carefully place the rabbit pieces into the hot oil. Stir to brown all over, remove and set aside. Add the onions and cook until soft. Stir in the 250-ml of water, tomatoes, tomato purée, vinegar, stock cube, bay leaves and salt. Bring the sauce to the boil, then return the rabbit. Simmer for about 1 hour or until the rabbit is tender.

Tips
Rabbit can be purchased cleaned and joited ready for cooking.

FATHSES

(Pheasant Dish)

Cut the pheasant at the joints to avoid splintering the bones. The hen pheasant is smaller and considered much tastier and tender when cooked.

Serves 4 to 6.

250 ml of water
250 ml of beer (any)
3 tablespoons of sunflower oil
half a teaspoon of ground cinnamon
2 bay leaves
1 teaspoon of salt
half a teaspoon of ground black pepper
2 pheasants, cleaned and jointed

Take a large saucepan and put in the water, beer, sunflower oil, cinnamon, bay leaves, salt and pepper, mix well then add the pheasant pieces. Cover, bring to the boil, then simmer for 30 minutes. Uncover and continue to simmer until the liquid has almost evaporated.

Tips
Pheasants can be purchased cleaned and ready to cook.

Basil

Holiday Cottage

Splendid views across the valleys
Mountains multi-coloured as high as heaven, kisses the
blue lit sky
Rambling, hiking through meadows, foot paths, rough terrain
stretch on and on, muscles aching just for pleasure, lets carry on
Lanes - wind, elevated, down ward slopes, left and right they twist
and turn, some are known as Roman roads
Birds chirping, cooing and singing like angelic voices, even like
church bells ringing, floating on a breath of air without a day time
care, roasting on a branch or two waiting for the night to pass
through
White sheep baa-in baa-in too and fro never stays still long
enough to say hello
Stare, stare never flinch, very crafty, bushy tail and
pointed snout, gingerly, gingery is that a fox I see taking
care not to be seen
Rabbit jumping, jumping, jumping there it bounces down
its barrow
Inside cottage large and spacious, exotic furnished
with old and new
Charming features, fire log burning what a
beautiful glow
Fresh air refreshing, peace and tranquil
lets stay forever, it looks better with fine
weather, please don't tell me I have to
go

savoury

cakes

Savoury pastries and cakes,
Fill the kitchen with a wonderful aroma when
deep-fryed or baked,
Spoon in those fillings and never mind how long it takes,
Your find it very easy making these simple shapes

bread

Breads are mostly made up of basic ingredients,
Mix it, knead it - cover and leave it - for just enough time
until the yeast ferments,
Get your stress out cause bread making's fun,
Drop into a bread tin - then take out the oven when the
crust is well done

pastry

&

ELINOKIPRIOS PSUME

(Greek - Cypriot Bread)

Bread is an important accompaniment to complete a Greek meal and usually torn apart by your hands rather than sliced. It has a crisp crust and a coarse crumb.

Makes 1 loaf.

750g of strong white flour
1 teaspoon of salt
1 small packet of dried yeast (7g)
1 pinch of ground cinnamon
2 tablespoons of extra virgin olive oil (plus extra for greasing baking tray)
enough warm water to bring the dough together
4 tablespoons of sesame seeds (optional)
1 tablespoon of aniseed (optional)

Sift the flour and salt into a large bowl, and then add the yeast and cinnamon. Add the olive oil and rub through the flour. Gradually add warm water and mix until the dough comes together. Turn out onto a lightly floured surface and knead for 5 minutes. Cover and leave to rise in a warm place for 1 hour. Knock the dough back and knead for a further 2 minutes, shape the dough into a round. Place the bread dough onto a lightly greased baking tray, cover and leave to rise in a warm place for a further 30 minutes. Using a sharp knife carefully score a neat circle about two thirds out from the centre on the top. Bake in a preheated oven on a moderate hot heat and cook until golden brown. To test the loaf, tap the bottom. If it sounds hollow it is done **or** carefully push in a knife, it should come out clean. Cool on a wire rack.

Alternatively, use half the dough to make a small loaf and the other half to make 15 bread sticks (*Paxamadoukia*). To make the bread sticks, roll the dough out into 20 cm (8-inch) long thin sausage shapes onto a lightly floured surface. Roll them in the sesame seed and aniseed mixture (if using). Bake until lightly browned, then turn the oven off and let the bread sticks dry out and turn crispy.

HALOUMORPITA

(Halloumi Cheese Bread)

I eat halloumi cheese cold, fried, grilled, baked, in a sauce and on a home made Greek style pizza, so what better way to eat it as in a loaf of bread. Delicious!

Makes 1 loaf.

750g of strong white flour
1 teaspoon of salt
1 small packet of dried yeast (7g)
1 tablespoon of dried mint
1 pinch of ground cinnamon
250g of halloumi cheese, cubed
125 ml of extra virgin olive oil (plus extra for greasing)
enough warm water to bring the dough together

Sift the flour and salt into a large bowl; add the yeast, mint, cinnamon and halloumi cheese. Add the olive oil and rub through the flour. Gradually add warm water and mix until the dough comes together. Turn out onto a lightly floured surface and knead for 5 minutes. Place in a lightly greased bread tin **or** baking tray, cover and leave to rise in a warm place for 30 minutes. Bake in a preheated oven on a moderate hot heat until golden brown. Cool on a wire rack.

ELIOPITA

(Olive Bread)

If you're an olive lover like I am - this bread is definitely one to make. It tastes savoury with the olives and slightly sweet with the onion. Nowadays, olives are so readily available it can be made at any time.

Makes 1 loaf.

750g of strong white flour
1 teaspoon of salt
1 small packet of dried yeast (7g)
1 tablespoon of dried mint
1 pinch of ground cinnamon
1 medium onion, finely chopped
150g pitted black olives
150 ml of extra virgin olive oil (plus extra for greasing)
enough warm water to bring the dough together

Sift the flour and salt into a large bowl; add the yeast, mint, cinnamon, onion and olives. Add the olive oil and rub through the flour. Gradually add warm water and mix until the dough comes together. Turn out onto a lightly floured surface and knead for 5 minutes. Place in a lightly greased bread tin **or** baking tray, cover and leave to rise in a warm place for 30 minutes. Bake in a preheated oven on a moderate hot heat until golden brown. Cool on a wire rack.

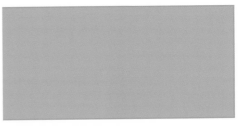

PITA

(Pitta Bread)

Some Greek food is served with pitta bread; it's the ideal accompaniment to dips, appetisers and barbecues.

Makes 12 to 15 large pittas.

1 kg of strong white flour (plus extra for dusting baking tray)
1 teaspoon of salt
1 small packet of dried yeast (7g)
enough warm water to bring the dough together

Sift the flour and salt into a large bowl, and then add the yeast. Gradually add warm water and mix until the dough comes together. Knead the dough for 5 minutes, cover and leave to rise in a warm place for 30 minutes. On a lightly floured surface roll the dough out flat to about 1 cm (1/2 inch) thick then cut into oval shapes. Place onto a lightly floured baking tray in a single layer. Sprinkle lightly with water and bake in a preheated hot oven for about 10 minutes or until they are slightly tanned. Remove from the oven and wrap the pittas in a tea towel to keep them soft.

Tips
For flavoured pitta bread, finely chopped fresh garlic and herbs can be added at the beginning of the kneading process.

SPANAKOTI

(Spinach and Feta Envelopes)

This dish is ideal for those who love to eat spinach and feta cheese together with the addition of the pastry envelopes they are ideal for taking on a picnic. The filling is delicious when used to stuff warm pitta breads.

Makes 6 envelopes.

filling mixture
1 medium onion, finely chopped
2 tablespoons of extra virgin olive oil
225g of fresh baby spinach leaves
1 egg
200g of feta cheese, chopped **or** crumbled
pastry
500g of plain flour
half a teaspoon of salt
half a packet of dried yeast (3.5g)
enough warm water to bring the pastry together
1 egg, beaten for brushing over pastry

Fry the onions in the olive oil until soft. Add the spinach and cook for 5 minutes. Add the egg, mix well and cook until set. Take of the heat and mix in the cheese then set aside to go cold.

pastry- Sift the flour and salt into a large bowl then add the yeast. Gradually add warm water and mix until the pastry dough comes together. Knead the pastry on a lightly floured surface for 3 minutes and divide into 6. Roll the pastry out into rectangle shapes. Divide the *filling* out equally and place in the centre of the pastry. Bring in the corners to the middle overlapping slightly to form an envelope shape, then brush the top with the beaten egg. Leave uncovered to stand in a warm place for 30 minutes. Bake in a preheated oven on a moderate hot heat until golden brown. Cool on a wire rack.

SPANAHOLPITA

(Spinach Roll)

These rolls are often made for religious occasions, often around Easter time. Nowadays we make them whenever we like. The roll must be placed onto a hot baking tray as this starts the cooking process so when it's cooked the pastry is crisp all over.

Serves 6 to 8.

1 medium onion, chopped
3 tablespoons of extra virgin olive oil
225g of fresh spinach, chopped
2 tablespoon of cous-cous
1 teaspoon of dried mint
half a teaspoon of ground cinnamon
half a teaspoon of salt
half a teaspoon of ground black pepper
pastry
750g of plain flour
1 teaspoon of salt
1 small packet of dried yeast (7g)
50 ml of extra virgin olive oil (plus extra for brushing and greasing)
enough warm water to bring the pastry together

Fry the onion in the 3 tablespoons of olive oil until soft. Add the spinach, mix well and cook until wilted. Add the cous-cous, mint, cinnamon, salt and pepper. Cook for a further 5 minutes then set aside to go cold.
pastry- Sift the flour and salt into a large bowl then add the yeast. Add the 50-ml of olive oil and rub through the flour. Gradually add warm water and mix until the pastry dough comes together. Cover and let it rise in a warm place for 15 minutes. Roll the pastry out very thinly into a large rectangle shape onto a lightly floured surface.

Sprinkle the mixture all over the pastry then roll it up into a large sausage shape, carefully twisting at the same time to finish into a coil shape. Place the spinach roll onto a lightly greased hot oven tray. Brush over with olive oil and bake in a preheated oven on a moderate hot heat until golden brown.

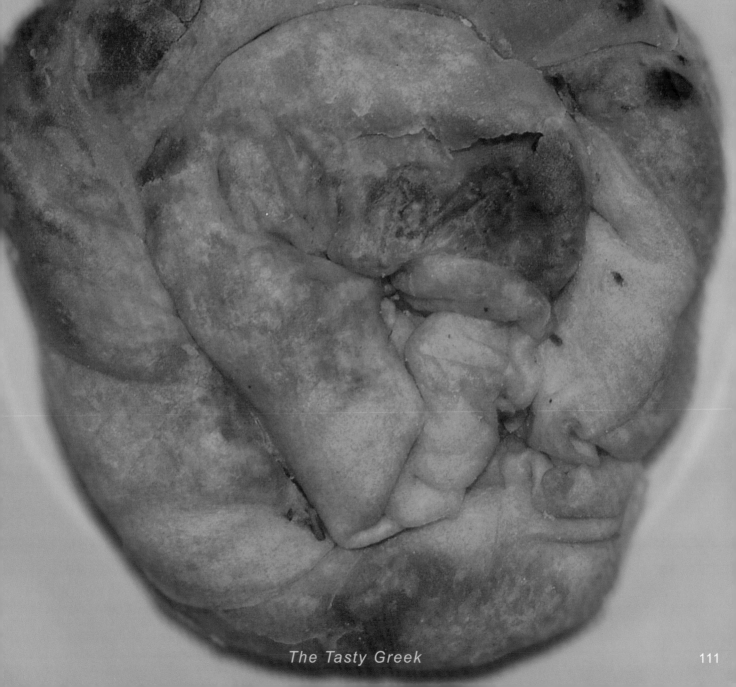

SPANAKIPITA

(Spinach Cake)

This recipe is very similar to the spinach roll but much more convenient in shape to take on picnics.

Makes 15.

filling
225g of fresh spinach, finely chopped
100g of cous-cous
100g of sultanas
half a teaspoon of salt
half a teaspoon of ground black pepper
half a teaspoon of ground cinnamon
1 teaspoon of dried mint
40 ml of sunflower oil

pastry
750g of plain flour
1 teaspoon of salt
1 small packet of dried yeast (7g)
50 ml of sunflower oil (plus extra for brushing and greasing)
enough warm water to bring the pastry together

Combine all the ingredients for the *filling* in a bowl, cover and set aside while making the pastry.

pastry- Sift the flour and salt into a large bowl then add the yeast. Add the sunflower oil and rub through the flour. Gradually add warm water and mix until the pastry dough comes together. Cover and stand in a warm place to rise for 15 minutes. Divide the pastry into 15 pieces and roll out flat into circles onto a lightly floured surface. Divide the *filling* out equally between the pastry and place in the centre. Fold the pastry over to look like a (D)–shape. Press down the edges with a folk and carefully brush over with sunflower oil. Place the spinach cakes onto a lightly greased baking tray and bake in a preheated oven on a

moderate hot heat until golden brown. Cool on a wire rack.

DAVE'S OUT OF HIS MIND

Dave, Dave you're a crazy dude
Plans to stay inside a goldfish bowl without no food
44 days and 44 nights
Just to see you up there gives me a terrible fright
Is it impossible for you to last?
This too most is one serious fast
I wonder - how can you put yourself through this
While we out here eat too much and call it bliss
Don't be disheartened when you're feeling the lows
Because I'm sure soon your be eating your clothes
At this moment in time I'm just passing through
But don't you worry Dave; I'll be back soon to check up on you
Good luck my friend and don't you give up
Its time for me now to flipping shut up

KREAS (or) HALLOUMI BOUREKIA

(Savoury Parcels - Meat or Cheese)

These nice little parcels are just as good for vegetarians as well as meat eaters. Ideal to pass around to friends when having drinks or as part of a mezethes.

Makes 15 parcels.

meat filling
3 medium onions, finely chopped
2 tablespoons of sunflower oil
500g of lean mince beef
4 tablespoons of fresh flat leaf parsley, finely chopped
1 teaspoon of salt
half a teaspoon of ground black pepper
1 teaspoon of ground cinnamon
1 teaspoon of dried mint
cheese filling
250g of halloumi cheese, grated
half a teaspoon of ground cinnamon
2 tablespoons of dried mint
2 eggs, beaten
pastry
500g of plain flour
half a teaspoon of salt
enough cold water to bring the pastry together
extra oil
sunflower oil for deep frying

Stage 1
meat filling- In a large saucepan fry the onions in the sunflower oil until soft, then add the mince beef, cook until browned, add the parsley and cook for a further 5 minutes, take of the heat and mix in the salt, pepper, cinnamon and mint. Drain and set aside to allow

the meat to go cold, while preparing the pastry.

OR

cheese filling- Mix all the ingredients together in a bowl and set aside while preparing the pastry.

Stage 2

pastry- Sift the flour and salt into a large bowl. Gradually add cold water and mix until the pastry dough comes together. Turn out onto a lightly floured surface and knead for about 2 minutes or until smooth. Cover and refrigerate for 10 minutes.

Take the pastry and cut into 15 equal pieces. Roll the pastry out very thinly into circles onto a lightly floured surface. Divide the *filling* out equally between the pastry and place in the centre. Folding the pastry over to look like a (D)-shape, then press the edges down with a fork. Keep the parcels covered under a tea towel to prevent the pastry drying out. Deep-fry the parcels in batches for about 30 seconds or until light golden brown. Drain on absorbent paper and transfer to a serving plate.

Tips
To make smaller parcels, cut the pastry dough into 20 equal pieces instead of 15.

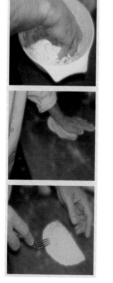 

THLAOUNES

(Easter Cakes)

Thlaounes are traditionally made and served during the Easter period. However, nowadays they are made and eaten all year round.

Makes 15 to 18.

filling
500g of mild cheddar cheese, grated
150g of halloumi cheese, grated
3 tablespoons of plain flour
half a teaspoon of baking powder
half a packet of dried yeast (3.5g)
half a teaspoon of ground cinnamon
1 tablespoon of dried mint
100g of sultanas
2 eggs, beaten
40 ml of warm milk
pastry
375g of plain flour (plus extra for dusting baking trays)
1 large pinch of salt
half a packet of dried yeast (3.5g)
1 pinch of ground cinnamon
1 tablespoon of sunflower oil
enough warm water to bring the pastry together
3 tablespoons of sesame seeds
2 egg, beaten

Combine all the ingredients for the *filling* in a large bowl. Cover and leave to rise in a warm place for about 1 hour or until the pastry is ready.
pastry- Sift the flour and salt into a large bowl, add the yeast and cinnamon.

Add the sunflower oil and rub through the flour. Gradually add warm water and mix until the pastry dough comes together. Lightly knead the pastry dough for 2 minutes or until smooth. Cover and leave to rise in a warm place for 30 minutes. Take the pastry and place onto a lightly floured surface. Roll into a long sausage shape, then cut into 15 to 18 even size pieces. Roll each piece out flat into circles and lightly dip the underside into the sesame seeds.

Divide the *filling* mixture equally between the pastry circles and bring 3 sides up towards the centre leaving a small opening on the top. Press the edges down lightly with a fork and spoon a teaspoon of the beaten egg in the opening on the top. Place the Easter cakes in single layers on a lightly floured baking trays and cook in a preheated oven on a moderate hot heat for about 20 minutes or until golden brown. Cool on a wire rack.

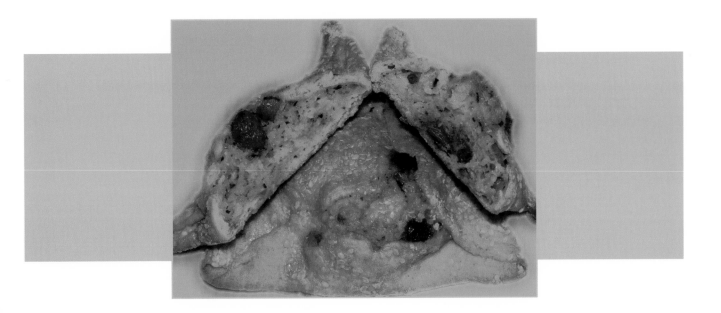

preserves

There's many ways of preserving,
My favourite is sweet things - I like serving,
Sweet tasting syrup dripping,
Dip your spoon in - then give it a good licking

sweet
pastry

coffee

A mysteriously dark bean, grown, picked, roasted, ground,
distinctively aromatic and strong tasting when brewed,
Drunk before and often after eating your food,
Served in small coffee cups - poured from a Gizfes,
Gives you an instant boost and thats what I like best

desserts

Exotic flavours make up these delightful desserts,
Enjoy the moment cause a little indulgence will never hurt,
So complete your meal with a special treat,
Nothing could be - better tasting than a delicious Greek
sweet

& cakes

Blend it, whisk it, fillo it and make it,
Toast it, bake it, sugar it and taste it,
Decorate, dissolve it, butter melting brush it - generously
sprinkle it,
Sticky, chewy, yum-yum in your tum - you know you can't
fake it

GLIKO GITHONYA

(Quince in syrup)

The quince will discolour while cutting and preparing but this does not affect them in any way when cooked. However, do check the quince as often as possible when cooking as one or two may soften quicker. In this case, remove and set aside.

Makes about 1 litre jar.

4 large Quince (peeled, cut into 8 equal parts and core removed)
water for boiling
syrup
650g of granulated sugar
700 ml of water
1 tablespoon of lemon juice

Place the quince into a saucepan and cover with cold water. Bring to the boil, and then simmer until just soft. Drain into a colander and set aside while making the syrup.

syrup- Combine the sugar and water in a large saucepan and stir occasionally over a low heat without boiling until the sugar is dissolved. Stir in the lemon juice and simmer for 10 minutes. Add the quince and continue to simmer for 15 minutes. Remove from the heat to cool. Bring to the boil, then simmer for about 50 minutes or until the syrup thickens slightly then remove from the heat (as the syrup cools it will thicken). Place the quince in a sterilised jar, pour in the syrup (strain the syrup if preferred) and seal. Best served chilled.

Tips
Any size jars can be used providing the syrup completely covers the quince.

GLIKO SIKES

(Figs in Syrup)

Figs are a tasty fruit and can be eaten hot or cold in many recipes. This is just another exciting way.

Makes about 1 litre jar.

10 small to medium size figs (slightly under ripe)
water for soaking and boiling
syrup
650g of granulated sugar
700 ml of water
2 tablespoons of lemon juice

Cut and remove the stalk end of the figs and pierce all over using a cocktail stick. Soak the figs in cold water for 1 hour. Drain into a colander and rinse under cold water. Place the figs in a saucepan and cover with cold water. Bring to the boil, then simmer for about 30 minutes or until tender. Drain into a colander and set aside while making the syrup.

syrup- Combine the sugar and water in a large saucepan and stir occasionally over a low heat without boiling until the sugar is dissolved. Stir in the lemon juice and simmer for 10 minutes. Add the figs and continue to simmer for 15 minutes. Remove from the heat to cool. Bring to the boil, then simmer for about 50 minutes or until the syrup thickens slightly then remove from the heat (as the syrup cools it will thicken). Place the figs in a sterilised jar, pour in the syrup (strain the syrup if preferred) and seal. Best served chilled.

Tips
Any size jars can be used, provided the syrup completely covers the figs.

GLIKO PORTOKALI

(Sweet Orange Peel)

This is a great way of using up the peel after eating the oranges. Preserving the peel makes a welcome sweet treat for any visitors. I push cocktail sticks through the rolled orange peel for quickness and simplicity, another method is to sew with a needle and strong thread through each roll until twelve rolls are done then tie the ends together - repeat this twice.

Makes about 1 litre jar.

4 large thick-skinned oranges with good skins (cut and remove a thin slice from top and bottom)
water for boiling
8 wooden cocktail sticks (soaked in water before use)
syrup
750g of granulated sugar
800 ml of water
1 tablespoon of lemon juice

Carefully grate the oranges all over to remove the very out side of the zest. Using a pointed knife cut an incision around the top and the bottom to loosen the flesh from the skin. Cut lengthways 6 strips then carefully peel away the pith from the orange flesh. Reserve the orange flesh for eating. Roll each strip of the orange peel up and push through and onto a cocktail stick (3 orange peel rolls to 1 cocktail stick). Repeat until all the rolls are done. Place the rolls into a saucepan and cover with cold water. Bring to the boil and change the water immediately, then repeat the boiling and draining process twice more. Cover the rolls with cold water and again bring to the boil, then simmer for about 45 minutes or until the rolls are soft and tender. Drain into a colander and set aside while making the syrup.
syrup- Combine the sugar and water in a large saucepan and stir occasionally over a low heat without boiling until the sugar is dissolved.

Stir in the lemon juice and simmer for 10 minutes. Add the rolls and continue to simmer for 15 minutes. Remove from the heat to cool. Bring to the boil, then simmer for about 50 minutes or until the syrup thickens slightly then remove from the heat (as the syrup cools it will thicken). Remove the cocktail sticks. Place the rolls in a sterilised jar, pour in the syrup (strain the syrup if preferred) and seal. Best served chilled.

<u>Tips</u>
Any size jars can be used providing the syrup completely covers the orange peel rolls.

GLIKO FILO DIZ BATIHA

(Watermelon Skin in Syrup)

This is a great way of using watermelon skin for a sweet to share with visitors at any time. It's hard to imagine what this dish will taste like, believe me when I say they are crunchy and delicious.

<u>Makes about 1 litre jar.</u>

half of a large thick-skinned watermelon with good skin
water for boiling
juice of 2 large lemons
syrup
750g of granulated sugar
800 ml of water
1 tablespoon of rose water
2 cm piece of cinnamon stick (1 inch)

Cut away <u>all the red flesh</u> from the watermelon skin. Reserve the watermelon flesh for eating. Peel off and discard the green hard outside layer of the skin. Cut into bite size pieces or strips. Place the skin into a saucepan and cover with cold water. Bring to the boil, and then simmer gently until the watermelon skin is <u>just</u> tender. Drain into a colander and rinse under cold water. Set aside to drain for 15 minutes and then place into a bowl. Pour over the lemon juice and mix well. Cover and leave to marinate for 2 hours. Place into a colander again and rinse under cold water, then set aside for a further 30 minutes to drain.

syrup- Combine the ingredients in a large saucepan and stir occasionally over a low heat without boiling until the sugar is dissolved. Add the skin and then simmer for 10 minutes. Remove from the heat to cool. Bring to the boil, then simmer for about 50 minutes or until the syrup thickens slightly then remove from the heat (as the syrup cools it will thicken). Discard the cinnamon stick.

Place the skin pieces or strips in a sterilised jar, pour in the syrup (strain the syrup if preferred) and seal. Best served chilled.

Tips
Any size jars can be used providing the syrup completely covers the watermelon skin.

RIZOGALO

(Creamy Rice Pudding)

This recipe is certainly a big favourite with the children. Creamy, tasty and filling it will soon put a glow to your cheeks.

<u>Serves 4.</u>

1$1/4$ litres of whole milk (2 pints)
2 tablespoons of orange flower water
100g of caster sugar
150g of pudding rice (short grain rice)
4 large pinches of ground cinnamon to decorate

Combine all the ingredients (apart from the cinnamon) in a large saucepan. Bring to the boil, then simmer gentle for about 40 minutes or until the rice is tender, stirring occasionally. Pour into 4 individual serving bowls and dust each with a pinch of cinnamon. Serve hot or cold.

GHALA MAHALIBI

(White Custard)

This custard is such a delightful dessert and the taste is unlike most custard. The recipe is simple to make and totally out of this world.

Serves 4.

725 ml of whole milk
3 tablespoons of orange flower water
4 tablespoons of sugar
3 and a half tablespoons of corn flour
4 large pinches of ground cinnamon to decorate

Combine all the ingredients (apart from the cinnamon) in a large saucepan. Bring to the boil, and then simmer gently for 2 minutes, stirring constantly. Pour into 4 individual serving bowls and dust each with a pinch of cinnamon. Serve hot or cold.

ROTHOSTIMA MAHALIBI

(Water Custard)

Custard made with water instead of milk, yes its true. This custard is very refreshing and made especially for the hot summers.

Serves 4 to 8

725 ml of water
4 tablespoons of corn flour
2 tablespoons of granulated sugar (plus extra sugar for sprinkling over the top)
500 ml of rose water

Combine the water, corn flour and sugar in a large saucepan. Bring to the boil, and then simmer gently for 2 minutes, stirring constantly. Pour into 8 wet small coffee cups. Allow the water custard to go cold and set. Turn out carefully into a large serving dish. Pour over the rose water and sprinkle generous with sugar.

SHAMISHI

(Semolina Envelopes)

Similar to the semolina slice the only difference is these are deep-fried and the semolina slice is baked. However, I'm sure you will not be able to resist making a few at some time. To prevent the pastry sheets from drying out, cover with a slightly damp tea towel until you are ready to use it.

Makes 12.

700 ml of water
2 tablespoons of caster sugar
2 tablespoons of rose water (plus extra rose water for sealing)
200g of semolina
6 sheets of fillo pastry
oil
sunflower oil for deep frying
decoration
60 ml of rose water
100g of icing sugar

Combine the water, sugar and rose water in a saucepan over a low heat until the sugar is dissolved. Bring to the boil and stir in the semolina. Simmer for 2 minutes, then carefully pour the mixture into a large baking tray. Spread the semolina out and set aside to go cold then cut the semolina into 12 pieces. Lay the fillo pastry sheets out lengthways and cut in half. Place a piece of the semolina in the centre of each piece of pastry. Brush the edges with rose water (this will help to seal) then bring in the corners to the centre overlapping slightly to form an envelope shape. Deep-fry the envelopes one at a time for 30 seconds or until light golden brown. Drain on absorbent paper and transfer to a serving plate. Sprinkle with rose water and dust generously with icing sugar.

GHALATOBOUREKO

(Semolina Slice)

If you like your desserts sweet then this one is definitely for you. It sets just like custard but much heavier and more filling so eat small portions at a time. To prevent the fillo pastry sheets from drying out, cover with a slightly damp tea towel until you are ready to use it.

Serves 6 to 8.

11/4 litres of whole milk (2 pints)
6 eggs, beaten
300g of caster sugar
2 and half tablespoons of corn flour
100g of semolina
melted butter for brushing and greasing
10 sheets of fillo pastry

syrup

150 ml of water
50 ml of rose water
400g of caster sugar
5 cm piece of cinnamon stick (2 inch)

Pour the milk into a large saucepan and bring to the boil. Meanwhile, mix together the eggs, caster sugar, corn flour and semolina in a large bowl, then carefully whisk in the boiling milk, stirring constantly (to avoid lumps). Pour the semolina mixture back into the saucepan and stir constantly over a low heat until the mixture thickens, then set aside. Take a large ovenproof dish and lightly grease with melted butter. Brush the top of the 10-fillo pastry sheets with butter. Lay half (5 sheets) over the bottom of the ovenproof dish overlapping the sides of the dish slightly and pressing down carefully to line the dish. Pour the semolina into the dish and use the remaining 5 sheets to cover the top of the semolina.

Roll inwards the overlapping fillo pastry onto the sides of the pudding. Brush the top with melted butter before placing into the oven. Bake in a preheated oven on a moderate hot heat for about 35 minutes or until golden brown.

syrup- Combine the ingredients in a saucepan, add the cinnamon stick and stir over a low heat until the sugar is dissolved. Bring to the boil then take off the heat. Let the syrup cool then remove the cinnamon stick. When the pudding is cooked, pour the syrup carefully all over the pudding allowing it to go cold and set before serving.

ARNARI BOUREKIA

(Sweet Cheese Parcels)

Using ricotta cheese in this recipe is best, not just for its superb creamy taste but it does not melt and run when heating.

Makes 15.

filling
300g of Greek ricotta cheese
2 tablespoons of caster sugar
2 tablespoons of orange flower water
half of a teaspoon of ground cinnamon
pastry
250g plain flour
1 large pinch of salt
enough cold warm water to bring the pastry together
oil
sunflower oil for deep frying

filling- Combine all the ingredients together in a bowl, cover and set aside.

pastry- Sift the flour and salt into a large bowl. Gradually add cold water and mix until the pastry dough comes together. Turn out onto a lightly floured surface and knead for about 2 minutes or until smooth. Cover and refrigerate for 10 minutes.
Divide the pastry into 15 pieces. Roll the pastry out very thinly into circles onto a lightly floured surface. Divide the *filling* out equally between the pastry and place in the centre. Fold the pastry over to look like a (D)-shape, then press the edges down with a folk. Keep the cheese parcels covered to prevent the pastry drying out. Deep-fry the parcels in batches for about 30 seconds or until light golden brown. Drain on absorbent paper and transfer to a serving plate.

XERODIANA

(Greek Puffs)

These little puffs are similar to a doughnut but have a denser texture when biting into them. Very nice all the same.

Makes about 40.

500g of plain flour
half a teaspoon of salt
1 small packet of dried yeast (7g)
3 tablespoons of orange flower water
enough warm water to bring a batter mixture together
sunflower oil for deep frying
caster sugar for sprinkling over the cooked puffs

Sift the flour and salt into a large bowl; add the yeast and orange flower water. Gradually add warm water and mix until it forms into a softbatter mixture. Cover and leave to rise in a warm place for 1 hour. Deep fry level tablespoons of the batter mixture in batches until golden brown then drain on absorbent paper and transfer to a serving dish. Sprinkle the puffs generously with caster sugar.

The Tasty Greek

MY SWEETHEART

My dear sweetheart
My mind is full of words only meant for you
To go on like this only makes me feel so blue
Like the oceans of the Mediterranean rich blue seas,
true salty blue, transparent blue, so blue like the sky so
beautiful
Reflections appear like an open book
Takes me back in time, we both took a glance into each
other's eyes
My heart skipped a beat - I tell you no lies
Wishing our lives would somehow entwine together
Knowing deep down inside feelings will last forever
and ever
No matter where life takes us, it's a must - you feel
the same way too
Never knowing how you feel towards me
Your smell, touch, taste - I can never grasp why my
dream will never last
This can only be a waste of time
I cannot wait for you to cross my path, sharing tender
moments, a giggle and a laugh
Isn't this just daft, knowing you will never be mine, mine, mine
It cuts deep like the oceans of the Mediterranean rich blue seas,
true salty blue, transparent blue, so blue like the sky so beautiful
Faze me not, I can take the pain
Believe me when I say, I will be just fine, fine, fine – with age and time

The Tasty Greek

BUSTOLAKI

(Sesame Seed Snack)

This is an excellent energy snack - full of goodness.

Makes 1.

sunflower oil for lightly greasing
75g of granulated sugar
3 tablespoons water
100g of sesame seeds

Grease a baking sheet with sunflower oil. Lightly toast the sesame seeds in a dry frying pan over a low heat until golden, remove and set aside. Combine the sugar and water in a small saucepan over a low heat. Swirling the saucepan gently until the sugar is dissolved. Increase the heat and cook until it becomes a slightly thick syrup and turns golden in colour. Add the toasted sesame seeds, stir lightly to coats (do not over stir, as sugar crystals will form when the snack sets hard). Immediately pour the mixture over the baking sheet and carefully spread to cover an even layer of about 6 mm (1/4 inch) thickness. Set aside to cool completely, then use a metal palette knife to lift the sesame seed snack off the baking sheet before braking into bite size pieces.

Tips
Do not touch the liquid sugar - it will be dangerously hot.

KOURABIETHES

(Short Bread Biscuits)

These biscuits are made at Christmas time to represent the gifts given to the baby Jesus. Also they are made and given out at weddings as a good luck gesture to the bride and groom.

Makes about 15 to 20.

200g of unsalted butter melted (plus extra for greasing)
3 eggs
60 ml of brandy
2 tablespoons of rose water
2 heaped tablespoons of chopped mixed nuts
2 heaped tablespoons of icing sugar
1 teaspoon of baking powder
600g of plain flour
(extra rose water and icing sugar for decoration)

Using an electric whisk or food processor. Add the butter, eggs, brandy, rose water, mix nuts, icing sugar and baking powder. Whisk for 30 seconds and then add the flour a little at a time to make a firm and smooth dough. Take small handfuls and make into pasty shape biscuits. Place in a single layer onto a lightly greased baking tray. Cook in a preheated oven on a moderate hot heat for 10 to 15 minutes <u>without</u> colouring the biscuits. Remove from the oven, while still hot sprinkle the short bread biscuits with rose water and plenty of icing sugar.

Tips
Alternatively, milk can be used instead of brandy.

KATAIFI

(Fine Pastry Cakes)

This pastry is somewhat different too most as it comes in long thin strips, knotted into bundles, folded together, bagged and often sold frozen.

Makes 12.

300g of kataifi pastry
melted butter for brushing and greasing
filling
100g of chopped mixed nuts
100g of pistachios nuts, chopped
1 teaspoon of ground cinnamon
2 tablespoons of caster sugar
2 tablespoons of rose water
syrup
250g of caster sugar
150 ml of water
75 ml rose water

Mix all the ingredients for the *filling* together in a bowl and set aside while preparing the pastry. Open out the kataifi pastry and carefully pull it apart into 12 bundles then lay out flat (being careful not to make any holes that let the filling fall through).
Divide the *filling* out equally and sprinkle over the pastry. Roll them up into a fat sausage shape and repeat this until all the pastry cakes are complete. Take a deep baking tray and lightly grease with melted butter. Arrange the cakes in a single layer and brush the top with the melted butter. Bake in a preheated oven on a moderate hot heat for about 20 minutes or until golden brown.
syrup- Combine the ingredients in a saucepan and stir over a low heat until the sugar is dissolved. Bring to the boil then take off the heat.

Pour the syrup down the side of the baking tray to about half way up the cakes. Serve warm or cold.

<u>**Tips**</u>
The kataifi pastry can be purchased from a Mediterranean green grocer.

THAKHTILO TO YINEKIA

(Lady's Fingers)

An elegant little sweet served with a strong Greek coffee when visitors come round.

Makes about 15 to 18 fingers.

pastry
250g of plain flour
a large pinch of salt
enough cold water to bring the pastry together
melted butter for brushing and greasing

filling
100g of chopped mixed nuts
1 tablespoon of orange flower water
1 tablespoon of caster sugar
half a teaspoon of ground cinnamon

syrup
150 ml of water
50 ml of orange flower water
200g of caster sugar

pastry- Sift the flour and salt into a bowl. Gradually add cold water and mix to form a firm and smooth pastry. Cover and refrigerate while preparing the filling.

filling- Mix all the ingredients together in a bowl and set aside.

Roll out the pastry very thinly onto a lightly floured surface then cut into 10 cm by 8 cm (4 inch x 3 inch) rectangle shapes. Lay a tablespoon of the *filling* along the centre of the pastry. Bring the long sides over to overlap and cover the filling. Press the ends down with a folk. Take a deep baking tray and lightly grease with melted butter.

Arrange the lady's fingers in a single layer and brush the top with the melted butter. Bake in a preheated oven on a moderate hot heat for about 10 minutes or until golden brown. Remove from the oven and set aside to cool slightly, while preparing the syrup.

syrup- Combine the ingredients in a saucepan and stir over a low heat until the sugar is dissolved. Bring to the boil then take off the heat. Set aside to cool slightly. Pour the syrup over the lady's fingers and leave to go cold before serving.

POURA

(Nutty Cigars)

A crisp, sweet and nutty delight to serve any time day or night. To prevent the fillo pastry sheets from drying out, cover with a slightly damp tea towel until you are ready to use it.

Makes 18 cigars.

filling
6 tablespoons of chopped mixed nuts
3 tablespoons of caster sugar
1 teaspoon of ground cinnamon
1 tablespoon of orange flower water

pastry
6 sheets of fillo pastry
melted butter for brushing over the fillo pastry

syrup
220g caster sugar
125 ml of water
100 ml of orange flower water

Mix the ingredients for the *filling* together in a bowl and set aside while preparing the pastry. Lay the 6-fillo pastry sheets out in front of you length ways and cut evenly into 3 (to produce 18 pieces of pastry). Brush the top of each piece with melted butter. Place a heaped teaspoon of the *filling* mixture nearest to you leaving a 2 cm (1 inch) border either side. Bring the sides in and roll forward until a thin cigar shape has been formed. Repeat until all 18 cigars are done. Brush all over with melted butter and place in a deep baking tray in a single layer. Bake in a preheated oven on a moderate hot heat for about 15 minutes or until golden brown. Remove and set aside while making the syrup.

syrup- Combine the ingredients in a saucepan and stir over a low heat until the sugar is dissolved.

Bring to the boil then take off the heat. Let the syrup cool slightly before pouring down the side of the baking tray to about half way up the nutty cigars. Let the nutty cigars go cold before serving.

VASILOPITA

(New Years Cake)

Vasilopita is baked for the Greek New Year. It is to celebrate St. Basil's feast day. He is the patron saint of Blessings and Wishes and is traditionally celebrated at New Year. A coin is rapped in foil and place in the uncooked cake, when the cake is cooked and cut the person who receives the coin is said to have good luck throughout the year.

Serves 6 to 8.

200g of caster sugar
1 tablespoon of baking powder
3 tablespoons of almonds, chopped
half a teaspoon of ground cinnamon
4 eggs
zest of 1 orange
150 ml of fresh orange juice
200 ml of milk
2 tablespoons of sunflower oil (plus extra for greasing baking dish)
600g of semolina
decorating
15 whole blanched almonds to decorate the cake
syrup
200 ml of water
75 ml of orange flower water **or** rose water
200g of caster sugar

Whisk all the ingredients for the cake together in a large bowl, leaving the semolina until last. Whisk in the semolina a little at a time to avoid lumps. Pour the mixture into a lightly greased ovenproof dish and decorate the top with the almonds. Bake in a preheated oven on a moderate hot heat for about 35 minutes or until golden brown.

syrup- Combine the ingredients in a saucepan and stir over a low heat until the sugar is dissolved. Bring to the boil then take off the heat. Let the syrup cool slightly before pouring over the cake. Rest the cake for 10 minutes before serving.

ELINIKOS KAFES

(Greek Coffee)

This coffee is always served without milk. It's a dark, strong flavoured coffee that gives you an instant boost. Pour the coffee when boiled a little in each cup at a time to finish with some froth, this we call *Gahimuki*.

Serves 2.

200 ml of water
2 teaspoons of sugar
2 heaped teaspoons of coffee

Pour the water into a very small saucepan (*Gizfes/Briki*). Bring to the boil then remove from the heat. Add the sugar and coffee and stir. Return to the heat and bring back to the boil. Just as the coffee reaches boiling point it begins to rise, take of the heat immediately to avoid spillage. Pour into 2 small coffee cups. Serve on its own, with a glass of water or with bread sticks to dip in (*Paxamadoukia*).

Tips
Greek coffee can be purchased from most Mediterranean green grocers.

This coffee is served in three ways :-
Unsweetened / Sketo
Medium sweet / Metrio
Very sweet / Gliko

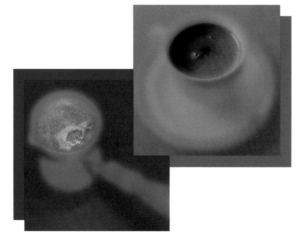

GLOSSARY

Here in Alphabetical order are some unusual ingredients,
cooking terms and useful tips to help everyone to
use and understand these recipes.

AUBERGINES: Otherwise known as egg plants, oblong and almost round in shape, purple is the most common variety with its shiny tough skin and slightly fibrous flesh is pale yellowish in colour.

BARBECUE: Place fire lighters or small dried twigs (kindling) at the base, then put on top the charcoal to create a mound or heap allowing small gaps to be able to light the barbecue. Once flames and smoke die down the charcoal should look greyish and glow red. Using a barbecue poker spread the charcoal evenly around the base. It is now ready for the food.

BEATEN: To beat is to mix by stirring. Whip using a fork or balloon whisk with a quick sweeping motion.

BOIL / BOILED / BOILING: Cooking any liquid rapidly to which it bubbles steadily, the temperature of boiling water is 100 degrees Centigrade/ 212 degrees Fahrenheit. The food is covered by the liquid, frequently in a saucepan/cooking pot on top of the cooker/stove to a high heat.

BROWNED: To cook until coloured and seal.

BULGAR WHEAT: Made using steam/boiling and cracking the wheat then dried. Available in fine or coarse grained.

CAUL - FAT: Knotted and stringy layers of fat taken from the lambs belly used for adding flavour and moisture and is white in colour.

CHEESE: *Cheddar* is a hard cheese, yellow in colour with different strength in taste from mild to extra mature, creamy texture which makes it a good all purpose cheese. *Feta* is a semi-soft curd and crumbly cheese. Creamy, soft and sour to taste. *Halloumi* is a semi-firm white cheese, salty and slightly minty to taste. *Ricotta* is a fresh, very soft light curd cheese, very creamy and milk like to taste.

CHOPPED: To roughly cut into bits or pieces.

COLOCASSI: *Colocassi* is a root vegetable, peeled it is creamy white and crisp to the sound when cut. Marinating and boiling softens the firm crunchy dense texture to a soft mushy pulp and semi-stringy flesh. Colocassi is similar in taste to a sweet potato.

COURGETTES: Also known as *zucchini*. Allow a tender little courgette to grow it will turn out into a large, tough marrow. Best when they are about 15 centimetre long, straight, firm and light green.

COUS - COUS: Made from semolina particles, slightly wetted or moisturised with salt water then sprinkled with fine semolina flour and rolled up into small pellets.

COVER: Anything that covers, as a lid, liquid, tea towel, top, cling film, foil, etc.

CRUSHED: To press, squeeze, grind or pound ingredients into small particles or to lightly crush is to use gentle pressure or little weight as not to ground completely.

DRAIN: To reduce, remove, and seep out or to draw off any liquid or moisture.

DRIZZLE: To slowly pour a small amount of liquid lightly or in a very fine stream over food.

DRY RED WINE: Dry red wine of a good quality is recommended as it produces best results when marinating or cooking food.

EIGHTH's (8th): To cut into eight equal parts.

EVAPORATE: To reduce the liquid by heating to concentrate the flavour.

FIGS: Small fruit of pear like shape, usually purple when ripe, soft to the touch, heavily seeded and sweet to taste.

FILINI: Small thin lengths of pasta.

FILO PASTRY: Also known as *phyllo* and *fillo*, the name comes from the *Greek phyllon*, meaning 'leaf'. Comes in paper thin pastry sheets and bought chilled or frozen. When using filo pastry cover with a slightly damp cloth to prevent it drying out.

FINELY CHOPPED: To cut into small bits or pieces.

FINE PASTRY: Very thin strands of pastry layered together.

GISFES / BRIKI: A small, long handled pot with a narrow top and broad lip.

GREEK COFFEE: Strong, dark and ground.

GROUND: As to grind or crush ingredients into fine particles, as in dried (herbs, nut, spices, etc).

KNEADING: To stretch, fold and turn over repeatedly until the dough becomes elastic and should look plump and smoothly rounded. Always knead dough on a lightly floured surface.

KNOCK THE DOUGH BACK: After the first rise the bread dough sometimes expands unevenly, to knock the dough back is simply to knead for a second time to expel the gas and allow the yeast to disperse better for an even and smooth dough.

LEAF BEET: Also known as *spinach beet* or *perpetual spinach*. Larger in size and a very hardy vegetable with thicker stems and takes longer to wilt when cooking.

MARINADE: A blend of/or a variety of ingredients used in cooking to add flavour and/or to tenderise food when soaked in it for any length of time.

MARINATE: To soak, pickle, steep in a marinade.

MEZETHES: Also known as *Mezze*, A combination of up to thirty different dishes and great to served to family and friends.

MIX: To blend or combine ingredients together into a single mass.

OKRA: Usually eaten green while still immature or slightly under-ripe. A ridged seed pod also known as ladies fingers.

OLIVE OIL: Extra virgin or virgin olive oil, these are the best quality used for its full fruity flavour obtained only from the first press. Choosing an olive oil is really a matter of taste.

OLIVES: *Green olives* are taken/picked unripe. *Black olives* are taken/picked when ripe.

ORANGE FLOWER WATER: This fragrant tasting liquid is used in many sweets and puddings. A process of distilling orange tree flowers or blossom.

PAR BOIL: To boil or simmer for a short time to partially/half-cook food.

PASTA No. 3: Long and large hollow tube pasta.

PASTA RICE: Known as *Orzo*, small pasta shaped like grains of rice.

PASTE: To bring to paste, as in a smooth texture.

PEEL / PEELED: To cut or trim away (skin, rind, etc).

PEEL OFF: To pull, cut away or remove in strips as of the top layer of skin.

PINCH: The amount of flavouring that can be picked up between finger and thumb.

PHEASANTS: Classed as *Game*, the term applies to birds and animals, which are hunted and eaten. Pheasant farming producers provide a supply all year (frozen). Best bought fresh between November and December. Hen serves 3. Cock serves 3 to 4.

PULSES: *Chick peas, butter beans, black eyed beans, broad beans.* Tin/Canned are factory processed and come ready to eat. Used in recipes for simplicity and convenience. Dried are uncooked and should be soaked in water over night before cooking. Boil rapidly for 10 minutes then simmer until tender. Always cook as directed on the packet.

QUARTERED: To cut into 4 equal parts or to cut in half, then in half again to have 4 pieces in total.

QUINCE: A large cooking pear light green-golden in colour. Firm crunchy flesh is very aromatic and is best used for jams, jellies and preserves.

RICE: Whitish, starchy seed with outer covering removed and polished, comes in long grain or short grain. Long grain easy cook rice has the starch content reduced providing short cooking time.

ROSE WATER: Distilled from rose petals, used in the same way as the orange flower water.

SALT TO TASTE: Add salt to the finished dish, mix well and taste.

SAUSAGE SKIN: Taken from pig intestines (pork skins).

SCORE: To cut into something but not to slice into pieces or slice through.

SEAL: To fry/cook the surface of meat in a hot pan or oven quickly for a short length of time until browned all over and to retain the juices or moisture in.

SEASONED FLOUR: Flour with salt and pepper added to it.

SEMOLINA: Made from the inner grain/part of durum or hard wheat. Yellowish in colour and granule like in texture.

SET: To set or cook until set is to seal the outside of the surface or to allow the food to become firm or firmer to the touch. Eggs, custard, meat, etc.

SHALLOW FRYING: To use a small amount of oil for cooking. A non-stick pan is a good way of reducing the amount of oil needed.

SHREDDED: To cut in fine or long narrow strips.

SIMMER / SIMMERING: Cooking in liquid just before boiling and bubbling only occasionally.

SIMMER GENTLY: To cook on a low to moderate heat.

SKEWER: A long metal or wooden (bamboo) pin used to hold meat, poultry or fish in shape during cooking.

SLICED: To cut a thin, broad piece from something between 5 mm to 10 mm in thickness.

SMOKED COD ROE: Fish eggs massed in the ovarian membrane taken from the female fish and smoked. Pinkish in colour and salt to taste.

SPINACH: Soft and tender dark green leaves, which should be handled carefully as can be damaged easily and crisp to the touch.

SPRAT FISH: Very small, silvery skinned fish of the Herring family.

SPRINKLE: Scatter thinly too lightly cover.

STOCK CUBES: Processed stock used for flavour, quickness and simplicity. Contains high levels of salt.

SUNFLOWER OIL: Polyunsaturated, readily available for culinary use and not too expensive to buy.

TAHINI PASTE: Roasted and pulped sesame seeds ready to buy in jars.

TENDER: To cook until soft, as to boil, stew, roast, etc.

TOMATOES: <u>Fresh</u> tomatoes used are *standard, plum and beefsteak*, ripe and deep red in colour. Plum tomatoes are especially suited to cooking, making tomato sauces and pur'ee. <u>Tin/Canned</u> are usually plum tomatoes factory processed and come ready to eat/use. Recommended in most recipes for convenience. Come whole or ready chopped. <u>Passata</u> factory processed ready to use. Consistency is between tomato puree and tomato juice. <u>Puree</u> concentrated tomatoes pulped with the moisture removed to a smooth thick paste. Also known as *tomato paste*.

TOP & TAIL: To remove, trim or cut off both top and bottom end.

TRAHANA: A coarse cracked wheat soaked in natural plain yogurt and dried into usually uneven size pieces. Sour to taste.

VERMICELLI NEST: Thin long lengths of pasta, which have been rolled together into nest like shapes.

VINE LEAF / LEAVES: The leaves of the grapevine used for wrapping food. A hand size leaf is ideal for the stuffing, they have a firm but fragile texture with a savoury taste.

WARM WATER: Is of hand hot only.

WEDGES: Cut in half, then cut each piece in half and in half again (8 pieces).

WILTED: To cook until soft, brake down or reduce in size.

YOGURT: Natural plain Greek yogurt, slightly creamy and white in colour. Alternative, unflavoured Greek style yogurt can be used.

NOTES

The Tasty Greek

NOTES

NOTES

The Tasty Greek

NOTES

NOTES

The Tasty Greek

NOTES

INDEX

RECIPES

A

B

C

D

E

F

G

H

K

POEMS & SONG

KREAS SOUVLAKIA (Meat Kebabs) Page 90